WRITING ROUTES

Writing for Therapy or Personal Development Series

Edited by Gillie Bolton

Writing for Therapy or Personal Development, a foundation library to a rapidly developing field, covers the theory and practice of key areas. Clearly exemplified, engaging and accessible, the series is appropriate for therapeutic, healthcare, or creative writing practitioners and facilitators, and for individual writers or courses.

by the same editors

Writing Works

A Resource Handbook for Therapeutic Writing Workshops and Activities

Edited by Gillie Bolton, Victoria Field and Kate Thompson

Foreword by Blake Morrison

ISBN 978 1 84310 468 1

Dying, Bereavement and the Healing Arts

Edited by Gillie Bolton

Foreword by Baroness Professor Ilora Finlay of Llandaff

ISBN 978 1 84310 516 9

Therapeutic Journal Writing

An Introduction for Professionals

Kate Thompson

Foreword by Kathleen Adams

ISBN 978 1 84310 690 6

WRITING ROUTES

A Resource Handbook
of Therapeutic Writing

Edited by Gillie Bolton,
Victoria Field and Kate Thompson

Foreword by Gwyneth Lewis

Jessica Kingsley *Publishers*
London and Philadelphia

'Reluctant I' (Kiteley 2005) on p.24 is reproduced by permission of Writer's Digest Books.
'The Mincer' (Schneider 2008) on pp. 45–6 is reproduced by permission of
Myra Schneider.
'Dr Shelley' (McAllister 2004) on p.48 is reproduced by permission of Shelley McAlister.
'Lucy' (Rudd 2007) on p.52 is reproduced by permission of Andrew Rudd.
Prose autobiography (Butler 2008, preface) on pp.59–6 is reproduced by permission of
Larry Butler.
'The Blue Gate' (Flint 2003) on p.105 is reproduced by permission of Rose Flint.
'The Year the Wall Came Down' (Sawkins 2008) on pp.110–111 is reproduced by
permission of Maggie Sawkins and *Brittle Star*.
'The Harper' (Redgrove 2006) on p.139 is reproduced by permission of Penelope Shuttle.
'Burning Want' (Murray 1998) on pp.140–1 is reproduced by permission of Les Murray.
'Diagnosis' (Hamberger 2002) on pp.154–5 is reproduced by permission of
Robert Hamberger.
'Dear Gillie' (Cartledge 2008) on p.178 is reproduced by permission of Patricia Cartledge.

First published in 2011
by Jessica Kingsley Publishers
116 Pentonville Road
London N1 9JB, UK
and
400 Market Street, Suite 400
Philadelphia, PA 19106, USA

www.jkp.com

Copyright © Jessica Kingsley Publishers 2011
Foreword copyright © Gwyneth Lewis 2011

Library of Congress Cataloging in Publication Data
A CIP catalog record for this book is available from the Library of Congress

British Library Cataloguing in Publication Data
A CIP catalogue record for this book is available from the British Library

ISBN 978 1 84905 107 1

Printed and bound in Great Britain by
MPG Books Group

Contents

Foreword

The recommendation to write can be dauntingly generalised. I like walking and have often found the trickiest part of the journey to be finding the beginning of the path. Once you know that your feet are on a way which has been followed by others, then it becomes much easier to pay attention to the surroundings and enjoy the view. As the poet W.S. Merwin has written, 'Stories come to us like new senses' (2008, p.62). Detailed maps are needed for where to start in creative writing and how to proceed. *Writing Routes* provides just such an atlas, essential information for anybody setting out on the adventure of self-discovery through words.

Telling your story straight can save your life but this practice of authenticity requires discipline and many drafts. The accounts of writing strategies in *Writing Routes* present many ways of setting out on the journey, along with a view of some possible destinations to intrigue and encourage. They have a practicality and experience which is sorely needed when dealing with difficult subjects, such as illness, loss and suffering. Overall, they show that we're never alone – even and, perhaps, especially, if all we have is words.

Many books have been published about the formal techniques of writing. Less attention has been paid to the way in which these methods interact with the discipline of trying to perceive and reproduce a personal reality. A true version of experience is the explicit subject of such writing but accuracy's also its most important formal constraint. It's certainly the reason why a newly apprehended truth can be both beautiful and liberate us from situations that have long baffled and pained us.

Sometimes it's said that art follows life, but I've found the opposite to be true. Where else but in the imagination do the first stirrings of desire form a tentative plan of action, for what might, much later, become part of one's biography? In writing, we're dealing with the prequels of decision, when the forms of our transformation have not yet solidified into fact, when there's still time to play with the possibilities. Small variations here can make all the difference later on. Be careful what you write, because you might have to live it.

Gwyneth Lewis
National Poet of Wales, 2005–06

Preface

Gillie Bolton, Victoria Field, Kate Thompson,
with a Postscript by Fiona Hamilton

In *Writing Routes* over 70 contributors give accounts of how they came to write a particular piece and why, and what it said back to them. They share how they found ways of transforming experience into writing, thereby gaining insight into themselves and their circumstances. These authors come from a variety of backgrounds and their routes into writing are equally varied. Some also facilitate others to write therapeutically, for personal development, or well-being, working in very different roles, for example: tutors, therapists, counsellors, supervisors, poetry therapists, lecturers, mentors, healthcare professionals, or writers in healthcare, schools, or well-being settings. A significant number use journaling, both for themselves and as a form of therapeutic intervention: personal writing can become a regular part of life, like exercise or meditation. Others describe how they were prompted to write for the first time by a life event, such as illness or wanting to preserve a moment. There is much overlap between these categories and this reflects the universal application of therapeutic writing. It is a dialogue with the self on a profound human level that transcends its particular time or place.

Each author has chosen a piece of their own writing, which they feel has been beneficial to them. And each one has carefully explained how they came to write it, in what way it was helpful to them. Writing these pieces was not always straightforward, many have been redrafted,

At some point you may arrive at the last chapter of this book. When the last chapter ends and you progress through the appendices through the index to the back cover, the act of reading will be coming to completion. Closing the book, you will glance at the back cover, which may have been where you started when you looked to find out something of what you were about to read.

And although the act of reading will finish, you may reflect on some of the writings here, you may dip into the book at some future date to refer back, to look again, to understand more deeply or from a different perspective. You may carry with you in your head some of the words, some of the tone of individual writers' reflections.

The writing was completed before you began reading, yet it too continues beyond its own confines. Here, writers have considered variously what happens when they write and this reflection will influence what happens next in their writing, and therefore in their lives. Strands of thought, feeling and meaning will nourish unfoldings of further inquiry and imaginative process. Reader and writer are unlikely to meet in person and yet their interactions, intangible and profound, are shaping things to come.

What pleasure there is in the creative word. What surprises, what liberties. How much like our lives, how unexpected, frustrating and glorious. And while it may be that we wish simply to dance our creativity without thinking too much about it, it may also be that in reflecting on how we use words to shape our worlds, we are privileged in noticing the ways in which creative writing inevitably involves creative reading of our experience, ourselves, our environment and our ways into the future.

CHAPTER 1

Getting into Writing

Edited by Victoria Field

People often discover the therapeutic potential of writing through trial and error. Many young people spontaneously begin keeping a diary or journal in their teens and there is often an impulse to create a poem at times of great joy or sadness. Others may attend a more formal writing class, with the intention of learning how to write poetry or fiction and discover, sometimes to their surprise, that they make many personal discoveries through writing.

Keeping a journal can be one of the safest ways into writing as there is no expectation that anyone else will see what has been written. Satu Nieminen describes two methods of journaling that have supported her. Alexandra Boyle found journal-writing prompts helped her on a journey to find herself and that redrafting a resulting poem gave new insights. Debbie McCulliss interrogates her journal to learn more about her self. She moves from journal-writing to life-writing and, like Alexandra, finds that by using less of the first person 'I', she gains distance from and a new perspective on her experience.

Conversely, having an insight into personal processes can also have an effect on more formal writing. Abi Curtis demonstrates how she writes a poem to capture elusive moments, drawing on published poetry and mythology as well as her own experience. Kate Compston shares a technique for coming to poetry from a new angle. Ray Russell found it easier to publish his stories when he stopped trying too hard. Sometimes, as Sarah Salway describes, changing aspects of one's writing can lead to changes in self-perception – as her fictional characters became more definite, so did she.

Writing a Journal: A Way to My Soul *Satu Nieminen*

I'm writing.
From the bottom of my soul
arise the fireworks of the words.

I've been writing journals as long as I've been able to write. During childhood I wrote about boys and the events of my life. As a teenager, I found my soul and shed tears while writing. Then I became pregnant and my journal took on a totally new meaning: I studied my changing body through writing. When I had the baby, I studied how to be a mother and how to act through that role. I write about my relationships in the pages of my journal. I will describe two techniques I practise in my journal.

Julia Cameron writes about morning pages (Cameron 2007). Morning is a difficult time for me and that's why I have 'night pages'. Every night in my bed I put two pillows behind me, take my glasses and my journal from their secret place. I have a few favourite pens I use. I make myself as comfortable as possible. Then I start. Usually I begin by writing about happenings. Next, I slide into the feelings. And maybe after a month, I can come to a conclusion about the theme I've been handling. This is a process described by Hynes and Hynes-Berry (1994). First, I recognise something that I want to study and understand. During the writing I can view the matter from many angles. I can compare my feelings and ways to act through writing and reading my words. I may write about the same stuff for a whole week or even a month. Then it loses its power. I can adopt a new way of thinking or acting or just accept the situation and stop fighting against it.

I write and I read. During this process I gain insight into my feelings. I learn how life's events have an effect on me and how I affect my own life. Sometimes I write few words. On other nights, the journal is burning in my hands and seven pages get filled. Writing in the evening helps me to forget the grief and difficulties of the day. I can leave them in the pages of my journal. So I sleep well. I can also pay attention to the happy things in my life. Every night I try to see something good and precious and end my writing with that. Sometimes I just read my writings and try to understand what I have felt or done. I can also check things in the journal's pages. It's also a calendar.

I learned to understand my burn-out through this process. I discovered my bad habits and I learned to change them. I understood that I was too kind and could forget to take care of my own rights and boundaries. The pages of my journal were the witnesses of my rage and passion.

5 October 1999

Today at work I just broke down! I started to cry. I just had a feeling that I cannot stand any patient and his/her problems. I feel myself restless, tired, sad and guilty. Guilty for the kids, why I haven't been with them more. Why I'm here with strange people trying to solve their problems instead of solving my own. Why I'm so busy all the time? This hurry kills me! And I feel anxious and confused. Something is inside of my chest. I just want to rest. Why have I so many thoughts that I should do this and that? But I haven't any strength to do those things. Is this all the illusion of the helper that this all cannot touch me? What happens to me? Am I ever capable of working as a mental occupational therapist?

4 November 1999
A poem
All those trees
side by side
giving support to each other.
I went alone
drift with the bad wind.

Of course there are times when I feel like I am blocked. I may feel that there is something inside me but I can't get a picture of it. Then I start reading poems. I pick up words and sentences from the books. I call this exercise 'circulation poetry'. After collecting words and sentences, I start to arrange them in a different order trying to figure out their meaning in my life as a whole poem. When I've finished, I name the poem. Every time I do this, the poem tells me what I have on my mind.

18 March 2008
A circulation poem
I want to be more open
more uncovered.
As open and bare as the bravest ones.
I let my strength to stream.
The strength that wants to cover.
The strength that is afraid of being strong.

People
curious and strange
crawling from their hollows
circle around, stumble against.
They look and they ponder, ask.
Enormous charging whips in the air:
You cannot beat her anymore!

Natalie's Golden Mantras *Alexandra Boyle*

I had 'returned to education' and completed an Access course in Theatre Studies. I was offered a place on a BA in Drama – and turned it down. I was 36; married for 13 years, with two school-aged children and I needed to work.

I discovered OCA (the Open College of the Arts) which offered accredited courses by Distance Learning. So I switched from part-time to full-time employment to fund my studies. The course I enrolled on, *Starting to Write*, was the next best thing to Drama. I had felt there was something in my writing trying to get out and I was going to find out what it was.

Enter Natalie Goldberg. Her book, *Writing Down the Bones* (1986), was included in my pack of materials from the OCA. My OCA manual was an A4-size folder which I worked through at home; Natalie's book was a compact paperback I shoved into my handbag for quick access.

It was soon followed by a journal, in which her mantras of giving yourself permission to write whatever you want, every day at a time to suit, as a warm-up for whatever you decide to write in the future – found their place. I faltered at first, struggling with my internal critic going, 'Oh we've started writing now have we? Got anything interesting to say, have we?' I had to keep Natalie's encouraging voice firmly in mind to support me, but I kept writing. Fifteen minutes a day soon turned into almost an hour – which I slotted into my day whenever and wherever was comfortable.

That was how my journal-writing started. Listening to myself enabled a much closer reading of others; those spaces in between creative and personal writing. Was that the 'something in my writing trying to get out'? Or was it drivel? A lot of personal writing can sound like that, I'm sure. But writing gives me a natural high I'm still hooked on and I've got eight years of journals. Or gems, as Natalie puts it in her chapter on 'Rereading and Rewriting' (Goldberg 1986, p.162), suggesting you let time put some necessary distance between you and your work. Then, objectively, you can find sections of writing which 'often glow off the page and are obvious' (1986, p.164). After years of dross, I can report that I have had a couple of those 'glowing off the page' moments, of which there may well be more.

And taking Natalie's cue, I have learned to adapt the exercise to any form of previous or current writing, finding that the lapse of time and the necessary distance, comes into its own when I'm standing outside of, rather than locked into, my work. The editor in me, coming from another angle, kicks in. This is an example:

Occasion
She'll sit on the train
gazing, wondering
if a wig will set tongues off
at the other end.

Glimpse her face
on dusty glass opposite, watch
the thought shape her mouth
into a smile going sideways,

then broad as her new fringe
is wide. People pick hats
for occasions, don't they,
why not a wig, this time?

She'll choose it carefully;
blue-black, slinky
to accentuate the eyes,
haunted no more.

Stick with the hat,
she'll tell herself now.
But this time
I'll be the new me.

Originally it had 'I,I,I', all over it. Re-reading it, I could hardly see anything else and immediately it struck me that 'I' didn't feel like that anymore. I switched to the third person.

Doing this showed me the following: I had moved on from the negative feelings which had driven the original piece. Altering the point of view required amendments elsewhere – and I was prepared to do this, to turn the poem around, because it mirrored my own 'turnaround'. It made me feel good. Finally, I could apply this exercise to other past/present/future pieces of writing; make them something else whilst retaining their meaning.

Creative writing led me to the journal – the journal led to that 'something trying to get out', which is the essence of me – it's what I'm trying to say.

Writing Yourself Forward *Debbie McCulliss*

Because words have mysterious and profound power, the process of writing can be life-changing and therapeutic. In various forms, writing has been part of my life for ten years. Experimenting in my journal took me on the wild ride of self-discovery. Learning craft ignited my writing.

Subsequently, I gave coherence, symbolism and meaning to my lived experiences and experienced better health and wholeness.

Keeping a daily journal allowed me to explore the intricacies of life and any beliefs, judgements, feelings that wouldn't lose their grip. After re-reading a journal entry, adding just a few sentences to my entries about what surprised me; what I wanted to further explore, or think about; what I was learning about myself; fuelled further clarity. This reflective writing and thinking prompted further questions, much like a conversation with a best friend. Questions that arose were:

- What feelings were evoked as I read each entry?

- What was I really wanting to say?

- What was I learning from my writings?

- What was changing?

- What was I coming to accept?'

One of the most profound questions I asked was, 'Why does it feel like I need to write to survive?' It took months for the answer to reveal itself. To find my voice came as a 'knowing' sensation, a kind of grace.

Writing about my intuitive, fear-based, or loving voice strengthened my ability to express myself, connected me to my body and trust its wisdom. I cultivated self-awareness and started to live more consciously when I highlighted my journal entries in different colours, moments of synchronicity and self-nurturing, areas of procrastination, times of transformation, shifts in thinking, actions taken, gratitude and insights. Patterns became evident with regard to words, personal or family issues, mood cycles and behaviour. Overlooked meanings surfaced. Journaling is accessible to everyone, and it's easy, whether with pen or computer. There is no right way to do it.

I'm also a strong advocate of writing life stories – memoir, personal narrative, poems, essays. By consciously reconstructing events and emotions, fragments of stories and parts of ourselves can be joined, aligned in time, and provide a wholeness, an 'aha' insight which can often foster wellness. This kind of writing is more refined than journaling, and it uses craft techniques: character development, dialogue, setting, back story, conflict and metaphor. The creative process aids in imagining possibility. Reading my work out loud additionally allows me to feel my writing, hear my voice and be sure my views and voice remain throughout the writing.

Journaling and writing life stories have a common focus on the 'I' voice. However, first person pronouns, if incessant in the work, can sound egocentric and become annoying to the reader. There are many times when the focus needs to be shifted away from the 'I'. Simple remedies include lessening the stream of 'I' and 'me' in the text, or writing from another point of view – second person (you) or third person (s/he). These can provide a psychological distance, and often a new perspective or an opportunity for change.

An excellent exercise is in Kiteley's (2005, p.20) book, *The 3 A.M. Epiphany: Uncommon Writing Exercises That Transform Your Fiction*. His 'Reluctant I' instructions read:

> Write a first-person story in which you use the first-person pronoun only two times – but keep the 'I' somehow important to the narrative… Imagine a narrator who is less interested in himself or herself than in what he or she is observing… Make sure the reader is not surprised, forty or fifty words into the piece, to realise that this is a first-person narration. Show the reader quickly who is observing the scene…

In 1979, I joined trekkers for a 33-mile hike of the Chilkoot Trail from Dyea, Alaska to Lake Bennett, British Columbia. I wrote the following, based on Kiteley's exercise:

> … The first day's eight-mile trek began at Skagway to the Dyea trailhead, ending a few miles later in a one-room log cabin at Finnegan's Point, the perfect place to bunk for the night, get warm, and dry everyone's clothes and boots. Weather conditions were cold and wet, even in the summer. This summer was no different; it was nippy and there were 18 inches of water and mud in many places…

> Sunday, clouds stayed at bay for the day's climb which began at 'The Scales', where prospectors from Gold Rush history had re-weighed their loads before heading to the summit… Despite hearts pounding from altitude and exertion, shoulders aching with the weight of backpacks, we continued up the

30-degree incline called the 'Golden Stairs', passing through snowy patches, mist, and fog. The changing landscape – sub-alpine firs through treeless alpine landscape to fields of boulders – offered proof that the summit was close. At the three-thousand-foot high summit, Americans and Canadians sang their respective national anthem. Despite cultural differences, all were unified in the exhilaration… Not only had I camped for the first time ever, my greatest sense of achievement came from undertaking this historic and memorable adventure.

I re-created this experience by studying disorganised, unlabelled photos and a diary written almost 30 years ago. The exercise taught me how important it is to let events speak for themselves, beyond the ego of the narration; how vital details are; and how to not overuse words – including 'I'.

Both journaling and life-writing offer different means to the same end: that is, expanding one's experiences into a personal sense of integration, meaning and possibility. As Ursula Le Guin, the fantasy novel writer, said (in Heffron 2000, p.6), 'It is good to have an end to journey toward; but it is the journey that matters, in the end.'

Writing 'Kingfisher' *Abi Curtis*

Two summers ago I was in a canoe travelling lazily along a small section of the River Frome with my partner, slipping over the skin of the water in the shade of willow trees, keeping watch for an elusive kingfisher. We didn't see one, but it seemed to me that the presence of something anticipated, something otherworldly, had impressed itself upon the landscape. I have always found it difficult to write from experience alone. At the same time, it's important for me to capture certain moments. On this occasion I felt the need to connect to the landscape, and this impetus came partly through wanting to deepen my understanding of my relationship with my partner. Such an experience feels like a memory even before it becomes part of the past. This produces a sense of melancholy in me, as though transience of every moment is pointed up by one of peculiar intensity. These are small, sweet griefs to be assimilated. Writing a poem eases that unsettling feeling.

Engaging with a personal experience, as well as a wider idea, or another writer, creates the necessary friction for me to write a poem. It is in this juxtaposition of elements, the effort to bring language, experience and images together that I feel most inspired. When I came home, I re-read Hopkins' famous untitled poem which begins with a kingfisher. The poem moves to capture the essence of the kingfisher – another self, part of the natural world, which is both elusive, and in touch with us. The first verse demonstrates Hopkins' use of the materiality of language in an attempt to 'get at' the feeling the kingfisher arouses:

> As kingfishers catch fire, dragonflies draw flame;
> As tumbled over rim in roundy wells
> Stones ring; like each tucked string tells, each hung bell's
> Bow swung finds tongue to fling out broad its name...
>
> (Hopkins 2002, p. 129)

The poem is also about finding what Hopkins sees as 'God' in the everyday. I'm not religious, but I'm struck by his ability to bring out the life in these simple experiences and to bring to life the individual words of the poem through his innovative arrangement.

Whilst thinking about this poem, I also researched the symbolic significance of the kingfisher. I found the Greek myth of Alcyone particularly moving. Alcyone's husband, Ceyx, dies at sea and she, not being able to bear life without him, drowns herself. The gods take pity (as they sometimes do) and transform them into birds. As birds they warn sailors of perilous rocks and are granted a short time, in winter, in which to hatch their eggs. The sense of loss and transformation that the myth offers provided another emotional dimension to my eventual poem and was not incompatible with the concerns of the Hopkins piece. Now I had three stories to juxtapose, contrast and compare.

Writing my poem involved several stages. First, I reflected on my experience, noting down impressions and images. Next I researched the themes of the poem in a wider context – looking at a Greek myth. Then I read the language of the Hopkins' poem closely. On a large piece of white paper (bigger than A4 – A3 or A2 works best) I wrote down language and ideas derived from these three sources, exploding the words over the page.

This became my raw material. I then re-combined the language into my poem, using the narrative of my own personal experience to shape its movement. This technique works for all kinds of sources – literary, visual and personal. It's about allowing different elements to fragment and then re-combining them in your own unique way, to access your personal experience through them, as it were.

The engagement with both the myth and Hopkins' poem allowed me the necessary distance to access the personal material – to provide a structure and a focus and relate my work to a wider literary context. As a result, and perhaps paradoxically, I was able to come closer to my experience, to use the writing to think through why it had emotional significance. I realised that a simple canoe-ride along a river was important because it highlighted the fragility and impermanence of such moments, and the importance of experiencing them fully. It also made me think that much of what strikes me as important is the absence or promise of something: that it does not necessarily have to be manifest to be recognised. It helped me to better understand my relationship, how partly relying on someone else for my well-being had unsettled me. My composition technique of filtering and considering experience through other cultural forms gives me the freedom to experiment with language and the focus to engage with my own personal experiences. There follows some extracts from my poem.

Kingfisher
… We watch for the kingfisher and find
her absence has left colour
                electric blue
          inside the damsel-fly
            gold-orange
     a feature on duck-beaks and berries
            viridian
      in the skin of the water-lily
          a cobalt
      through the willow-shadow
         a black-silver
from a bottle lodged in algae.

Alcyone has drawn this for us
treasuring her winter-eggs   the iridescence
        of her losses…

... I remember the gods catch envy from all of us
and it magnifies
like a reed half under a river.
I want to see the features of your face
but pause before I speak in case
                          you look back.

Poems Invite Us to Write Them *Kate Compston*

A recipe for warming my life when it has grown cold, or for enlivening my writing when it has become stale, was given to me during a course in Transformative Studies undertaken a few years ago. Because it was an MA course, it had a large research component – and, yes, I groaned and was afraid, because I had always understood research as being about statistics, and 'out there' material, and all the ways of asking questions which show up my logical incompetence. But here I learned that research can be qualitative and personal and particular, and that the very best questions can arise from re-imagining accepted ideas. Indeed, research is just that: re-searching, re-perceiving, looking from a new angle, making a prism through which to see life in different colours. So the recipe was that standing things on their heads (or doing a head-stand myself) offers a particularly dramatic fresh slant.

I started using this suggestion in various contexts. And one day, someone (probably a creative-writing guru) said the simple words, 'I invite you to write a poem'.

Flipping this over, in a way that was now becoming increasingly exciting to me, I wondered what it would be like if a poem invited me to write it.

And, instantly, I knew that this mirrored, and gave a voice to, my experience. It offered a much needed antidote to something that had made me angry some years earlier, when another creative-writing guru suggested ways of 'capturing' poetic insights and then making language 'submit' to their expression. Such a process sounded, with its war-like metaphors, far too driven, arrogant and stereotypically masculine to be useful to me. My experience of writing, and my desired (if not always attained) experience of living, was less aggressive, more flowing, more receptive to what the cosmos/god/the muse has on offer in the present moment.

The perception that a poem might be waiting for me to find, receive and write it was one of those eureka moments – rather like the instant recognition of truth I experienced when I read somewhere that the earth is responsive to our tread upon its feeling skin…

So I had my first line: 'Poems invite us to write them.' It was not in any way difficult to continue, though I do have a self-given technique for writing much of my poetry, which will not suit everyone. For me, it offers a release, whereas for some it would be a prison. I usually like a guiding discipline, such as a certain metre, or so many lines per stanza, or a rhyme-scheme, or assonance, or (most frequently) half-rhyme; because this guiding discipline gives me a sense of containment, whilst also tempting out the 'knowings' of my unconscious mind.

Let me explain this a little more fully.

If I write entirely 'free' verse, I tend to find myself putting down what I already think, i.e. what is in my conscious mind. But if I set myself the task of, say, writing with half-rhymes, and thus need a word that is going to be harmonious with another according to a certain pattern, then the sound tends to come first, and the idea follows on. And that follow-on idea comes from a deeper place than anything my surface mind can suggest. In this sense, something new is released.

Of course, I do revise. Constantly. I think about what my unconscious mind has thrown up and try to make it comprehensible to others. Or I find a better sound.

Memories and associations surface in the writing, as they did in this poem. I had not intended, when I started, to pay homage to a poet friend (now dead, alas) who told me that she received poems through the palms of her hands. Nor did I intend to use the thought, from the Coptic Gospel of Thomas (v. 30), that we find the Christ if we turn stones or cleave wood. Here, of course, I am not finding Christ, but finding a poem.

And yet, sometimes those two discoveries are not so far apart. Writing poetry always seems to take me onto holy ground. The process is so mysterious, such an epiphany. Especially if I'm standing on my head!

And naturally, it remains a question for me, and for the reader, quite whether 'poems', here, are to be understood literally or metaphorically.

Poems invite us to write them.
They are rarely insistent. They simply whisper
from old stone walls where lizards laze, from
trains lumbering through tunnels, and from the lisp the

dried leaves offer as they meet, embracing.
We must listen deeply or we will not hear them.
We are their servants, but are busy dicing
our lives away for fripperies. 'O come!'

say the poems, 'hold out your hands
and we will brush your fingers, cross your palms.'

Our deafness is not cruel. Simply, our minds
are not attuned, do not glide in these realms

any more, not since we were children, when we heard
the poems more purely, yes, could even taste them…

Shall we become children again? It's time we cared
more, cleaved the wood, released them.

Relaxing into Writing *Ray Russell*

My admiration for certain authors has always meant that I have tried in my own writing to inhabit similar territory to theirs. I have not attempted to imitate them for fear of simply producing pastiche, but there have been aspects of their style, technique and even philosophy that I have believed to be models that can only have a positive influence. I have always been aware that I have never quite succeeded in my aspirations.

And then, last year, I was invited to contribute a short story to an anthology and for a number of reasons I decided that if accepted I would publish it under a pseudonym. I immediately found this idea liberating and sat down and simply wrote the story as I might have tried to tell it verbally. The writing flowed very easily and I enjoyed the whole process. I came back to the first draft a few days later to correct infelicities and alter the pacing, and I was happy with the result. It was submitted, accepted and published, and then I went back to trying to write as I had done before.

After the pseudonymous story was published a number of reviewers mentioned it favourably, and I have to admit that I was rather annoyed that I couldn't bask publicly in the small amount of praise that I had received. I re-read it and decided that although I was pleased with the story, it wasn't quite what I was striving for.

I decided that I would repeat the exercise. After all, the writing had come easily and I had enjoyed myself. Once again it worked out well and on submitting the new story to a magazine it was accepted.

I tried not to think too much about the implications of this, but I went on to finish a number of stories using this technique, and even revisited an old novel and dissected it to form a simple short story that had been at its core.

As I sit back now and look at the couple of dozen stories I have written in the past year I realise that many of the ideas I was previously concerned to force upon my work have surfaced naturally, even though I was not aware of this at the time of writing. It seems that in the past I was giving these ideas too much consideration, and the story-telling itself was neglected. Now, using my new technique, all of the interests and concerns I was trying to communicate through my stories are somehow present without me trying to push them to the forefront. Characteristic themes, ideas and predilections surface in my writing with little conscious effort from me.

It is rather painful to admit that my work had previously been over-written and full of affectation, but this is the only conclusion I can draw. By relaxing (forgetting my rather unrealistic aspirations and not worrying how other people will receive my work), I have enjoyed not only the process of writing but the results, and I am now happier with and more confident in my abilities.

Happily Ever After ... And Then What? *Sarah Salway*

Ten years ago, on a trip to China, I took a walk on my own in a big city and got lost. I understood none of the signs and there weren't the clues – car parking, office buildings, chain stores – that I normally relied on to guide myself around strange places.

All I could do was carry on walking until I came to a big hotel, and from there, eventually, traced my way back to where I was staying. But that lack of my usually keen sense of direction seemed to mean I also lost the solid ground on which I walked. I had even had to cling on to a lamp-post on one corner, not wanting to take another step.

It was the same sense of panic I felt when, three years ago, I lost my internal map once more, but this time in my personal and private life. I could travel along fine, on the surface even successfully in some areas, but I wasn't sure where I was heading. Or if I would know the end when I got there. Or even if it was where I wanted to go. The ground had shifted under me so I felt as if I was skating over my life, unsure of its meaning. One of the ways this manifested itself was in my work. I couldn't find a foothold for myself in my writing, and so took little pleasure when people admired my stories for their cleverness. I worried that I was using gimmicks to mask what I really wanted to say, but I wasn't sure what that was.

In most of my stories, I allowed the reader to decide what happened to my characters at the end. I always argued passionately, and mostly successfully, that ambiguous endings were part of my writing style so when, in a journal therapy session, it was suggested that I try alternative endings for a piece I had just finished, I resisted.

Of course, resistance can be a useful tool to pinpoint where something important is hiding so the first time I gave a new ending to an existing piece of writing I had thought finished, I had to force myself to push on sentence by sentence as I took the characters on from my original deliberately vague conclusion towards one that was definite. As I wrote the final lines, it was exhilarating to realise that the place they had reached was the one I'd decided they should get to, not the reader. The idea that I could carry on and try different end scenarios was first of all frightening, and then liberating. Anything might happen.

I turned to a poetry sequence I was in the middle of, *The Unfit Mother*. This consists of a series of persona poems about a marriage in which the wife is a shopaholic. Following my usual process, I had already written the last poem in the sequence before I'd completed the whole thing. It was a haiku expressing how Caroline feels when her addiction means she's no longer able to look after her child:

Stabs of missing her
sink into Caroline's skin
bone white lullaby

With my new found interest in changing the ending, I wondered what might happen if Caroline took responsibility for herself, rather than just giving up. In the prose extracts I wrote to complement the poems, this is exactly what I had her do:

> My name is Caroline. I had an addiction and I recovered. This is not the end of the story. It never is. Just as it isn't the end when Cinderella marries Prince Charming. They still have to work out a way of sharing the duvet, coping when he snaps at her before his second cup of morning coffee, or she takes just too long getting ready before they go out...

And as I went back and fixed new endings on more of my already published stories, I knew I was doing more than playing. By adding a definite ending, or changing the ending, I had to go back and think about what the whole story meant for me, and what I wanted it to mean to others.

With *The Unfit Mother* sequence, the biggest surprise to me was how extending the ending allowed me to show more compassion not just to Caroline, but her husband too. It became less of a bitching session between the two narrators because Caroline was no longer a passive victim. This made the whole sequence more powerful and rounded. It seemed it wasn't just Caroline who had accepted responsibility, but me as writer too.

Once I started to look at my endings, I realised how many of my main characters were left waiting for other people to act on him or her. And from this, I could explore what this was saying about how I felt about my own life at that time. 'There has to be some blood in the cookie to make the Gingerbread Person come alive,' Margaret Atwood has said in answer to an interview question as to whether her work was autobiographical (Boddy 2006). It works the other way too. Sometimes the gingerbread man is so busy running away that you can't always see where the blood is until you read your own work, sometimes long after you have written it.

Life and fiction, fiction and life. To take control of the ending, I had to be more direct in my meaning. This is what I want you to feel. And I knew I needed to do this in my life as well. What I hadn't been aware of was how scary it was for me to be heard directly, not to cloak my meaning in metaphor or ambiguity. It's partly how I've been brought up

– nice children should be seen, not heard. Saying directly what I wanted also brought with it the possibility of rejection.

However, leaving the ending vague in life, deliberately keeping things open for people to interpret in whatever way they want, can be even more dangerous. It took me back to that Chinese street where I – literally – didn't know which way to go and walked in random directions, waiting for someone to come along and rescue me. I didn't want to live like that anymore.

My writing has shifted hugely since I started being more deliberate about my endings. It's as if the whole story is coloured a little more brightly. Rather than just offering it up to the reader, 'What do you think happens here?', I'm now saying, 'This is what happens, right or wrong. There can always be another ending, but this is the one I've picked.' It means I stand behind my stories more because I have thought about what they mean. I have put more of my beliefs in them – after having to think long and hard about what I do believe in. 'Finding your own voice as a writer is in some ways like the tricky business of becoming an adult,' writes Al Alvarez (2005, p.23).

And, of course, it leaks into my own life. Through digging into my fiction, I have been able to dig into my own life, and be first, less scared about things ending, and second, more willing to take responsibility for myself instead of waiting for a magic someone to come along and 'act on me'.

As my character, Caroline, finishes the monologue I've extracted from above: 'This is not the end of the story. But at least, now, for me it's a start.'

CHAPTER 2

Forging Identities

Edited by Kate Thompson

All the contributors in this chapter show a curiosity about themselves and others, seeking to understand and describe in writing how identity is forged and changed by encounters, experiences and environment.

Dreams can provide much information and even guidance. Freud (1899/1997) described them as 'the royal road to the unconscious' (p.25). Juhani Ihanus and Angela Stoner use this idea as the starting point, though not allying themselves with Freudian orthodoxy, and write about their dreams. Through their writing they strive for understanding of their own identities and lives. Tim Metcalf refers to dreams and daydreams as he explores the relationship of people and landscape as metaphor in the development of a moral identity.

Tim Metcalf, Shirley Serviss, Andrew Rudd, Myra Schneider and Shelley McAlister show how they use the stages of crafting poems to develop ideas and viewpoints on identity. Many of these show development over time – Myra Schneider's 'Mincer Character' began 12 years earlier, Andrew Rudd's poem evolved over months. Andrew Rudd and Shelley McAlister both explore the identities of people who have impacted on them and through whom they come to new understanding of themselves. Shirley Serviss shows how writing poetry can make universal the particular human experience and so reach out to others. Cheryl Moskowitz illustrates how we are touched by contact with other people, however transitory the contact is.

Writing Dreams *Juhani Ihanus*

Writing my dreams started almost simultaneously with my first poems at the age of 15. I noticed some of my favourite poets had been the torch-bearers in the twilight or dawn realms of dreams. Poe, Coleridge, Baudelaire and Rimbaud had managed to bring forth precious dream fragments. Soon I found many others and was fascinated by the literature attached to dreams.

I began to do dream work, writing everything that I can from the dream as soon as I am awake. I try to keep to the archaic, bizarre, fuzzy and funny logic, but wakefulness adds rational tones. Even the immediate account of a dream is already secondary and elaborated. Sometimes I have woken up at night to write, but usually I write in the morning. I make notes of dreams to be related and reflected. Later, I can process some of this raw material into a 'story', usually a (poetic) prose piece or a prose poem, if the material insists on being realised. Raw material contains more personal experiences, while the 'story' is more communicatively rewritten, 'literary'.

This dream writing process has varied in intensity and length. There have been long periods without any dream notes. Then suddenly, dreams can be forceful, wonderful, horrible, crazy and wise, and I will get caught in their grip. Writing dreams can begin wherever and whenever. I encounter attractive/repulsive expressions, whimsical shifts of the normal order, conflicts and provocations, unthought-of connections, orientations, or transformations, and curious visions or sense combinations that demand (free-floating) attention and spur self-reflection. Not only metacognitive, but also 'metaemotional' skills (understanding by feeling how you have felt, how you feel and will feel) can develop through attending to dreams.

I was linked to dream interpretation and to neuroscientific dream research, at the University of Helsinki. Although I appreciate dream theories, I do not actually interpret my dreams according to any theoretical formula. On the contrary, I negotiate with my dreams about personal meanings, and I can even re-story and readjust a theory on the basis of my material.

Most dream theorists say that all the characters, emotions, environments, situations, happenings and plots are staged and directed by the dreamer. That does not prevent me from enjoying the touching and illuminating artwork of dreams.

I was writing this in Vienna, the city of Freudian dreams. I went on dreaming my way in spite of analytic 'revelations'. I dreamt about a book of articles.

> *August 18, 2008*
> The book had Latin-origin and multilingual words. Every word referred to some other language. I remember that I read the book openly. One word in particular caught my attention, because it set the tone: it was 'hibernation'. Does that word exist? Of course, it exists in the world of that book. One article had several series of colour photographs about decomposition. I sensed that the approach was somewhat profane, still sublime: the stories of Christianity were here seen as part of universal-poetic decomposition. Instead of the Crucified, there were in the altar erected and lying breads at different stages of decomposition. I saw the split skulls of animals and the corpses of insects, as fossils in the transparent pieces of amber. A human being was mentioned only in a minor footnote. I was waiting for some esoteric Latin sentence to surface, but there was no revelation. Towards the end, the book was page after page full of brownish-grey photographs of frail spider webs. Water drops were trembling in those webs with numerous shells of insects in different pale shades of light. The text curved with them and with ever more fading and evaporating letters to its end. I cannot remember the end, because it came so suddenly that I could not recall it.

Such texts are playful and open to questions. For example, I often start by asking, why exactly this dream right now in this way. The dream then offers me answers, such as:

You are reflecting on writing for that English work. You
wonder whether you will manage to contribute to the web
of foreign-language words, especially when you are a kind of
hibernator in the tension field of writing. You have some high
ideals but you are not sure whether they will be nourishing,
since your human situation is very fragile and you are getting
older. There will be no revelations from above, and your fate
is to decompose like every other being of nature. You feel
that your words reduce to a minor footnote. However, you
sense a lot of poetic and visual beauty in the frail web of
letters, so why not write in the joint enterprise, why not let
the text curve to the end without any clear-cut method. Just
trust, while still trembling between living and dying, that the
dream will carry you on.

Even in one such short dream story there are several other routes and
existential-experiential topics. I can make use of units and configurations;
I can split and combine characters, objects, emotions, fantasies, thoughts
and memories in the web of dreams. Dreams not only explain the past
and the day's residues but they anticipate something. Through writing
dreams I open up for surprise. Dreaming is personal learning is change is
transformation. Dreams are not a store of ready-made wisdom products.
I can ask my dreams about the unknown; they expect that.

I guess dreams have invented the 'virtual'; they can connect to the
sensual-flowing mind-brain-bodies amid the noise of information. By
writing I can become resistant to the worst forms of soap-opera dream
fabrication rampant in the media. Personal dreams have not been
branded; they tend to run over programmed horizons, seething, and
carrying over forbidden emotions through censorship:

August 19, 2008
I have imported dolls filled with the dope of hope through the
Customs. The worst crime was, however, that I undermined
monuments and institutional buildings with my dreamy
eyes...

What have I learned from writing dreams? For example, that my memory is alive, there are vistas and eras to be further explored, my secure knowledge is deceptive, and my implicit knowledge is expanding. I emerge from my dreams as recreated and rewritten, even when only as a drafted mini story. Dreams do not solve the problems of my existence, but by letting them inhabit it, I have tuned into new dimensions. Dreams are writing me as I am writing on them, making meaningful differences. Writing dreams is action, experiential working through the unclarity of knowing, in the cloud of unknowing. This imaginary-poetic exploration makes the dreamer more aware of the 'adventurous heart' and its enjoyable languages.

The Whole Picture *Angela Stoner*

This dream emerged after I had told myself I would sleep on a problem. I had got involved in a dispute between two very dear friends and felt deeply unhappy. I was making myself ill over the situation and was considering whether to see a therapist about it. That night I had a very vivid dream. I scribbled down what I could remember of the dream.

Later in the day, I decided to work with it. I looked at my scribbles and began rewriting the dream in the present tense, and trying to feel my way back into the dream as I wrote. As I was writing, I remembered more details from the dream. This is what I wrote:

> I have paid a lot of money for a private consultation with a therapist. I am shocked to discover that he is expecting me to stay with G out in the corridor. He is not even going to be with us. All he asks us to do is spend time contemplating a picture. I am so angry that I am beside myself with rage. How dare he lump me with G, who is a depressed alcoholic who does nothing to help himself? I need individual attention. This is what I have paid for. I am so angry that I hardly pay any attention to the picture which is obscured by a red mist. I hear a voice, perhaps it is the psychiatrist's saying that the whole picture is a map.

As I write this, my resentment and anger become almost tangible, and I can feel the picture frame in my hand. As I write the words *out in the corridor* an awfully traumatic childhood memory surfaces of being left out in the corridor of a hospital when I was about four and had refused to stop crying. I am very shaken to remember this again so vividly. Is my mind confusing my current distress with this painful childhood experience? I'm not quite ready yet to explore this in writing, though. In fact, I put my pen down. After a while, I pick it up again. I read through what I have written and decide to give it a title 'The Whole Picture'.

I realise that I am fascinated by the picture…the picture I couldn't even see clearly in my dream. After all, the psychiatrist had said that the whole thing was a map, and we are often told to 'look at the bigger picture'.

What if the picture could speak? I decide to give the picture a voice by writing out a short imaginary dialogue between the picture and me. To do this I need to try to stop thinking about what I am writing, but just allow my pen to move over the paper. I need to be playful enough to believe that the picture has a voice and something to say to me and will do it through my pen. Very quickly as I do this, the picture takes over and does most of the writing. I decide to start with my emotion from the dream, a very childish and sulky rage. Interestingly, as I write, I begin seeing the picture properly. This is an excerpt from the dialogue:

> **Me:** I don't understand why I should look at you. I paid money for a private individual session. I can't even see you properly. And I don't know why he's lumping me with G, who is not at all interested in personal development.
>
> **Picture:** Well, he is the one who is looking at me, and taking the advice, so for my money he seems most committed to personal development. You seem a huge fool to me, not even taking the advice you paid for! Why don't you try looking at me?
>
> **Me:** But I can't even see anything. It's all blurry, obscured by a red mist.
>
> **Picture:** Keep looking at me. Look. Calm down. The red mist which obscures me has grown from your rage, jealousy and self-obsession. You create the mist, and you can disperse it. It

takes time to clear. Let your emotions pass through you and clear away. Stop being obsessed with yourself. Calm down. Be patient. Calm down. Look at me. Look at me. What do you see?

Even as I am writing, in my mind's eye, the red mist is rolling away and I am back in the corridor, holding the picture, but less angry and able to see the picture in my dream and to look at it properly as it emerges. The picture begins to look like some Japanese scroll, and contains a mountain, a river, a tree and a Buddha. I am astonished at how vivid these images are. They are oddly calming. I continue writing:

> **Me:** I see a mountain, a tree, a river and a Buddha. The Buddha seems to be laughing uncontrollably.

Simply writing this out has changed my mood completely. When I began writing, I was feeling angry and resentful. Now I feel that I have somehow discovered an inner picture which I can access to give me perspective and calm. It is also exciting that even as I write, the dream picture is becoming clearer and clearer in my mind's eye.

As a result of this dream, I began taking up meditation again, in particular guided visualisations, feeling that this would enable me to access my 'inner picture'. For about a month, I spent time every day letting the images from the dream picture become clearer in my mind, and then allowing each image in turn to 'speak to me' through automatic writing. In this way, the writing process became a form of meditation in itself, and gave me access to inner wisdom. Through writing, the picture in my dream became an inner therapist, and enabled me to see the bigger picture about the situation I was in, so that I was less blinded by the red mist of my emotions.

Letter to a Stranger – Processing the Momentary
Cheryl Moskowitz

This is a letter to the girl who saved my life.

> Imagine you are waiting to cross a busy road and you step out when you think it is all clear to go but then someone – a stranger – pulls you back because a car you haven't seen

is coming around the corner fast. And you know that this stranger has saved your life, but you don't know how to say so.

This is what happened to me to make me write the piece that began the way I started it above. It was just a moment. She pulled me back and I suppose I was more than a little embarrassed. We both waited until the lights had changed properly and then we both went on to wherever we were going to. So easy to ignore or to forget except that it was a moment that shook me and threatened to leave me shaken.

I did not write anything, or even think I would, until a few days afterwards. I was having my lunch, thinking about something entirely different, and the image of me on the busy road and the girl pulling me back came washing over me again making me blink my eyes hard, and shake my head trying to rid myself of the sensation. There was nothing for it. I had to get out pen and paper and write. This is the first line that came to me: *This is a letter to the girl who saved my life...*

Why a letter? I knew it was not going to be a letter in the conventional sense, that is, not a letter I could ever send. I would not see the girl again. I knew nothing about her, her name, how old she was, where she was from. We had not exchanged any words that day, only that one moment at the crossing. There was no real story as such except the uncomfortable feeling I'd been left with and I certainly didn't feel like dwelling longer on that feeling. In a way it was having no story and no knowledge of the person I was addressing that made this form the right one and made writing something, anything, possible. Instantly I was in my imagination, where I needed to be to write.

> I'm trying to remember you clearly now but I can't. I'm going to say you were wearing pink. A pink jacket, one you love. You wear it probably even when it's warm enough not to need a jacket. Like how warm it was the other day. The sun was shining on both of us. I started to go and you must have seen your whole life flash before your eyes. Thought you might have to see something that would haunt you for the rest of your life. That was the second you grabbed me...

Thinking back on the incident had made me close my eyes and this was like writing with eyes shut. Picturing things that might not have been there, probably didn't happen, or can't have been known. *A pink jacket.* Was it pink? Was she even wearing a jacket? *One you love.* So, this girl has favourite items of clothing, pieces of music and, no doubt, people. In the writing, in my imagination, I could discover them all. *The sun was shining on both of us.* I'm not sure whether it was or wasn't but I chose the weather that seemed to fit. The page can be your film set. Do you need it to be raining? Make it rain. You are the one telling.

A few months ago I was in New York with my eldest daughter. We were sitting on a train waiting to leave New Jersey to go into Manhattan. The doors were held open while the train idled on the tracks. Then something happened, it was only a moment. I heard a noise and saw a commotion on the platform. A man had fallen down the stairs. He was hurt badly, maybe even dead. My witnessing of the event was only a moment but it was a shocking one and I was not going to rid myself of it easily. Several days of re-living that moment and finally I managed to write something, another letter, this time in absolute certainty that the person to whom the writing was addressed would never see it.

> This is a letter to you, the man at Journal Square Path station in Jersey City seen at around eleven on the morning of the 22nd of August 2008. Friday. It's always eleven isn't it? I mean when the serious, momentous things happen. Bad things, good things…
>
> (Moskowitz 2010)

Like my previous piece it was born out of a real moment that had happened but the telling was full of imaginings: it had to be. I was writing a letter to a man I knew nothing more about other than what I had witnessed in that terrible moment itself. Though the letter was addressed to him it would be my feelings that would determine what was in it and how it was written.

Using 'you' to address the man felt somehow arrogant, maybe even irreverent given the circumstances. However, the direct address assumes a certain intimacy and helped enable me to give voice to the strong emotions I was experiencing.

Our days are filled with moments. Most of these never get written and usually that doesn't matter but sometimes it feels like it does. Sometimes a moment happens that causes a jarring, a disturbance, a confusion or such an explosion of feeling that you know you will have to re-live that moment in nondescript jolts and shivers, shakes of the head or blinks of the eyes unless you find a way to process and make sense of it in some other way.

Writing in this letter form works best when not only the moment itself is strange and out of the ordinary, but also the subject to whom the writing is addressed is a stranger. The people I was writing to were not known to me but imagining they were, or at least that I could know more about them than I did, made it finally possible to comprehend, process and begin to make sense of the powerful impact of the moment.

The Mincer Character *Myra Schneider*

About 12 years ago in a workshop I found myself describing a childhood memory of the mincer being clamped to our enamel-topped kitchen table. I was surprised at the emotion which welled up: that heavy sense of sunlessness I frequently experienced from the age of eight because women seemed to spend much of their time in drudgery. I remembered too the vehemence with which I used to say to myself: surely there is more to life than this? I kept my notes as I knew they contained the seeds of a poem but I didn't start developing them because a sixth sense told me that recreating the scene in the kitchen wouldn't lead to the kind of poem I wanted. Several times during the next ten years the mincer idea came into my mind but nothing sparked.

Then in January 2007 I suddenly found myself thinking of the mincer as a character. I'm not quite sure what triggered this but I think it was something I'd read. It led to a very brief scribble in my notebook: 'The Mincer. that solid body – aggressive – what do I want to say about it? – mincing myself. Do flow-writing.' Two weeks later I wrote a note on the computer about the character of the mincer: how it came into its own when its body parts were fitted together, that it was a character not to be messed with and had never heard of the country of perhaps. This was followed by a straight descripton of a mincer, its parts and how it operated. In order to be accurate I dug out from the back of a cupboard a mincer I'd not used for years and put it together. Then I went into thoughts about cooking and what the mincer symbolised for me. I developed the character using details from the mincer I'd observed.

By now I was really excited by the 'person' I'd brought to life and I knew I'd found the driving force of the poem. I began to think of form and rhythm and had the sense that couplets and short statements would fit the mincer's character. From then on the poem came fairly easily. The first six verses established the uncompromising personality. The opening verses, the form and tone guided me as I picked out details I needed from my childhood. Intuitively I used repeats of 'It meant…' which seems to me to emphasise those deep-seated feelings I'd uncovered back in the writing workshop. The way was now paved to express how I asserted myself to combat the mincer and everything it symbolised. Drafting the poem was satisfying, fun even and it was also empowering. I think its humour and irony reinforce the underlying emotion.

The process I went through with 'The Mincer' illustrates to me that simply relating potent personal material is not necessarily the most effective way to present it. In this case building up the personified image enabled me to transform my material into a piece of work which carries a charge.

The Mincer

Fitting the handle to the twisting blades
of what might be stomach or heart, is a feat.

When it's fully assembled the heavy innards
can be viewed through the gape in the head.

A screw buttons the rings of the mouth. Once
the table's in its grasp, thanks to metal wings,

anyone can see the mincer is not to be messed with.
It's as familiar with holding back as the black dog

with two heads, has never heard of the country
of perhaps. Neither subtlety nor beauty

are words in its language – there are half a dozen
for mastication. I manage to avoid this character now

but once I saw it being packed on Wednesdays
with dry chunks cut from the Sunday roast

I can't tell what she hears,
whether the fierce little sounds
she makes are telling me
pleasure or pain. I play
high on the keyboard

and I think she is joyful,
I think we are meeting
over impossible distance,
vast waters, as seagulls
exchange their shrill cries

This began to feel like a poem. The stanza shape 'grew' out of the material, a natural form for what I had to say. But it didn't feel finished – the image of the seagull, though pretty, did not quite fit. I put the poem to one side.

A few months later I was on a poetry course at Aldeburgh. Gillian Allnutt set us an exercise on the shingle beach: to find an object, then write a short poem in the first person using short, self-contained lines. I discovered a taut rope stretched across the pebbles, going down into the sea. At the top it was fastened underneath a boat, at the bottom it disappeared into the water. This rope fascinated me – it crossed a boundary, it linked two worlds. I began to write. An hour later, this had become:

I am tied to the earth
But I vanish into water.
Shadow in the sand.
Guiding the boat from one element to another
My whole length is a boundary marker, and the sea breaks
     over me.
The boat runs over me.
I am a bridge across shingle and sand.
I am tight enough.
My interstices are black with oil, then green with weed.
I am anchored, I can take the weight.

Using the first person provokes an identification, an exploration of self. New things started to appear which were not about a rope.

I think there is a particular psychological state in this stage of writing – a suspension of the interpretive faculty, a willingness to use writing to explore, without necessarily understanding what I'm writing about. It feels risky – a journey into the unknown, into something like a trance. And yet, as a writer, I am keenly aware that this is the most rewarding place. The words on the page will tell me things I need to know.

The piece now seemed to have energy, but, not knowing how to develop it further, I put it to one side for about six months.

It gradually dawned on me that these two texts were linked: the rope could be the metaphor I had been looking for in my encounter with Lucy. I wove the two pieces into one. After a few more drafts, and some critical feedback from friends – this is how it came together:

Lucy

When Lucy's hand taps out
the rhythm of my music,
I call to her with melody
and chords, keeping pace
with her moving hand.

I can't tell what she hears,
whether the fierce little sounds
she makes are telling me
pleasure or pain. I play
high on the keyboard

I think we are meeting.
I am a rope fastened
to land which vanishes
into the sea. Black oil
in my fibres

then green algae. Anchored
I am tight enough
I can take the weight.
I think we are meeting.
I think she is joyful.

So this is the published version (Rudd 2007, p.15). The poem still feels important to me in ways that I can't really express – it tells me things about myself. The long, slow process of finding the exact word, turns out to be a process of discovering the self. I realised that I could actually *do* what I had described in the poem: to communicate heart to heart without words, to be confident in that encounter. These were things I already knew objectively and intellectually, but in making the poem they became a deeper part of who I am.

Dodging Rednecks with a Grudge *Tim Metcalf*

I was walking one evening as the new moon set. I was talking to myself as usual, and thought the scene before me might make a line in a poem that could carry meaning. Here the new moon could be a light that represents a new idea, but unfortunately it is setting, not rising as I had hoped. This reminded me of our many human failures, war and environment being the themes of the evening. I recalled another line I had long been carrying around in my head, 'Drought, and the western district weeds blow in', that one day would form the kernel of a poem in which I could express my frustrations with some of my countrymen and their attitude to the land.

My part of Australia, the far south coast of New South Wales, has been in drought for most of the last decade. Conditions on my bush property are excellent for plants that normally live out west of the Great Dividing Range, where the drought is worse and the vast Murray-Darling River, pumped dry for irrigation, is now almost dead. The eastern coastal ranges are the destination for our internally displaced drought refugees whose western farming lands have collapsed. Unfortunately some of these people bring with them destructive behaviour they consider 'traditional' rights, but which have contributed to the environmental wreckage, such as shooting native animals, grazing or clear-felling the bush, and leaving hunting dogs free to roam in packs.

The result of my walk was that two lines became associated in my mind. Once I had this basic progression in place, I could start building a poem to house it. I arrived at many individual elements by combining observation and association. For example, galvanised tin, or corrugated iron, is a recurring visual theme of rural Australia. The words 'Southern

Cross' are frequently seen in the outback as the company name on the galvanised vane of the windmill bore-pumps. The constellation they are named after is a patriotic symbol of the pioneering spirit of rebellious freedom in nineteenth-century Australia. Our day-dreamers are still galloping through a land whose largely imaginary freedom was predicated upon the disempowerment of the native peoples.

The leaves of some plants are a soft grey, so I associated these with metal. The daisies that arrived with the drought are a strikingly attractive but harsh flower, so they represent both contrast, and the struggle for beauty in the bush. They are bright yellow and everlasting: they can be picked ready-dried for the table.

Sound is another medium in which to associate observation and meaning. Corrugated tin can be described as fluted, and in the context of my poem singing can also refer to ancient aboriginal storylines. The strongly onomatopoeic word 'flat' evokes the desert landscape as well as echoing a gunshot. I imagine that if there are still dreamtime spirits they will be heaving a long sigh of relief when the white refugees leave their desiccated lands, and this sigh reminds me of wind.

An alternative technique is to place images together to create a picture. In my poem a clutch of kangaroo's fur lies beside a spent cartridge for effect. The image is created out of ordinary objects, fluffed by what must be the wind, forming a suggestive relationship. In order to acknowledge man is not the only killer in the bush, I changed the word 'clutch', which evokes being grabbed by a bullet, to an eagle's 'talon-ful'.

The process of gathering connections and writing them down draws me into the complexity of the world. I become pleasantly and productively entangled in the possibilities raised. Condensing my thoughts and feelings into few words requires clarity of expression. Formulating the poem in its technical detail is mentally satisfying: the focus required creates a relaxing distraction. Perhaps it is like playing a game of Scrabble: win or lose there is nevertheless a collection of words that do fit together.

The title of my poem was developed last. As the east coast mountain range is also called the Great Divide, this seemed an obvious place to look for an interesting and relevant metaphor. The great divide between me and the destroyers of nature? The wide range of opinion? The title I settled on, 'East of the Divide', reflects the geographical reality, and quietly brings in an association with those eastern philosophies that embrace gentleness to all creatures.

Working over my poem to make it flow smoothly and sound better to my personal ear, it begins to work on me. The poem asks me questions: What am I about; why are you writing me; what do I say about you? These people who annoy you so much, how do they see you? Why does it madden them that you want to leave the animals and plants in our native forest alone? The potential implications of my self-(or selfish) analysis are not always good, and nowadays I discard poems that are not going somewhere positive, or at least looking for some way out. Here I have expressed my disappointment in a concise way that I can share with others if I wish. Perhaps it is a trifle cryptic, or 'poetic', but then I don't want to be visited by rednecks with a grudge!

In trying to find a positive way to step free of my frustration, this poem helps guide me to some kind of personal release. By combining images and ideas and associations it takes on a richness of its own, a dark beauty despite itself that shows us the world is infinitely complex, and that in writing it down we discover our interconnectedness. This opens for us many doors to forgiveness: of others, and of self.

East of the Divide
Drought and the western district weeds blow in:
a galvanised foliage, a fluted iron singing,

fluffing by a cartridge a talon-ful of 'roo fur.
The Southern Cross is a flat piece of tin.

Bush daisies rise dry but everlasting,
bristly in their yellow rustle-skirts.

There's a new moon at the end of the road
but it's falling behind the trees. Through them

from far-off deserts an ancestral wind
is breathing a long-time sigh of relief.

Writing Barefoot *Shirley Serviss*

My writing is often generated from a need to understand something I am experiencing, to make sense of it or meaning from it, or to work through the emotion the experience evokes. While the act of writing – putting words on the page – can be healing, what is most healing for me is not the writing in itself, but the work of crafting it into a poem or essay.

Writing within the constraints of a form means I begin playing with the words; choosing them for their sound as well as for their meaning (using alliteration, rhyme or rhythm for example). I may change details for this reason, or for symbolic purposes, or exaggerate for effect. As I do this, I become more and more distant from the initial experience or emotion. The piece of writing becomes something unto itself and is no longer a part of me. This allows me to leave behind the difficult experiences or feelings that inspired the writing and move on.

Natalie Goldberg (1986) describes this process very well in one of her short essays: 'We Are not The Poem'. She says that instead of freezing us on the page, writing frees us, and I've found that to be true. When I write in a particular genre, I find that the work takes on a life of its own. I often surprise myself by discovering things I didn't know, or going in a completely different direction than I intended. Metaphors may emerge. Solutions may reveal themselves. Difficult subjects or experiences may become humorous.

I'm often asked how I can read something so personal in public and my answer is that it's no longer about me. By using a form, the writing moves beyond simply being cathartic into a more public realm. It becomes a piece about the end of a relationship or the death of a parent, not the end of my relationship or the death of my father. This is partly what allows the reader or listener to engage with the piece. 'You're telling my story,' other stepmothers said to me about my first poetry collection *Model Families* (1992). 'I didn't know anyone else felt that way.' When my poems about my father's dementia were aired on CBC radio, listeners called the station requesting copies because the poems were about their experience with their ageing parents.

I believe that what we do by writing about the difficult experiences in our own lives is to give people permission to write or speak about their own. The writing is not only healing for the writer, but also for the reader or listener.

One of the methods I use to allow myself to write about something personal is to use the second or third person rather than first person. 'She' or 'You' can admit things that 'I' cannot. Another technique I use is metaphor. 'Barefoot' is an example of both distancing ploys. It was written after a long period of thinking about relationships following the painful end of a seven-year love affair. Reflecting on my behaviour in terms of footwear gave me insight into the roles I had played with various partners and helped me to realise I wasn't being authentic.

At the time I wrote the poem, I was exploring the possibility of entering into a new relationship and thought I had figured out how to conduct myself to avoid being hurt. The poem had its own ideas and chose to end quite differently. I was surprised by the ending and by the insight it revealed and am still trying to live into that understanding. Through the writing of the poem, I realised the impossibility of being open to love if one is guarded and the inevitability of experiencing pain if you are open to love.

Barefoot
Next time she'll wear her work boots
with scuffed toes and ragged laces,
not be quite as careful to keep from
tracking mud on the floor.
No high heels to contort her
into someone's fantasy. Nor army boots
to stomp all over him or running shoes
ready to flee. But work boots so she
can be herself: a bit battered and bruised,
a bit dirty, but protected and strong.

She'll retire the ballet slippers she wore
far too long, as she tiptoed through relationships,
matching her steps to various partners,
wearing costumes too constrictive,
acting roles choreographed by others.
She's tired of being so flexible,
bending backwards to accommodate,
pirouetting around trying to please.
Weary of leaping into the air

hoping someone will catch her.
Picked herself up too many times
to trust that anyone will be there.
Wants to keep both feet on the ground.

But does love work this way? Can it penetrate
her steel toes? Or must she wear sandals –
be open and vulnerable? Even go barefoot,
hoping by now her soles are tough enough
to withstand the inevitable stones.

CHAPTER 3

Writing the Self

Edited by Victoria Field

The 'self' can be defined in various ways and has lots in common with identity – see Chapter 2. It refers to what is essential about us (our 'essence'), what makes us particular or individual and also what we experience as the 'sum of our parts'.

Life events and our ancestors play an important role in forming a sense of self. Larry Butler found connections between a renegade uncle and his own role as a 'black sheep' in his family. He also alerts us to the fact others may have viewed events differently, something that may only be apparent when writing is made public.

Francesca Creffield engages with the multiple nature of the self through visualising different personalities as strangers on a bus and documenting possible conversations. Dominique De-Light takes on personalities and characters in her writing that enable her to express feelings that might otherwise be repressed.

Rosie Alexander describes the niggling feeling that something isn't right which can occur when we 'lose touch' with ourselves. She found that persevering with freewriting eventually yielded a single sentence which led to a poem and a renewed sense of connection. Sue Glover

Frykman also used freewriting, but with music and the environment as added stimuli, to gain insights into aspects of herself that were neglected or not fully acknowledged.

Kathleen Adams, in contrast to the freewriting approach, decided to take her health as a theme and wrote about it daily, working through the alphabet. This process led to positive changes in how she took care of herself.

Finally, who is the 'self' doing the writing? Briony Goffin describes her frustrating search for an authentic writing voice and a technique that helped her find one. In Sandy Hutchinson Nunns' piece, we learn how Transactional Analysis (TA) enabled her to distinguish between the self who wrote the piece and her own multi-dimensional self reading and reflecting on it. For a general account of TA see Stewart and Joines (1987).

Black Sheep in the Family *Larry Butler*

The following prose autobiography is included in the introduction to my collection of poetry: *Butterfly Bones* (2008, preface). I sent it to the publishers (Two Ravens Press) as a joke at the suggestion of a friend. The publishers decided to include it in place of the usual biographical notes. The genesis of this writing came from a Lapidus conference during a role-play workshop where we dressed up and improvised. A character gradually emerged through the spontaneous interactions: I was a pimp managing two whore houses and a troupe of rent boys in a mid-western town in the USA. I hadn't a clue how or from where this being emerged from my unconscious – until the following day at another workshop on family histories, I chose to write about my uncle whom I only met a few times when I was very young. We were encouraged to write non-stop for ten minutes. Afterwards, while reading aloud to a partner, I realised the connection with the earlier role-play. I use the word 'black' throughout this piece because 'black sheep in the family' was, and still is, a common expression with white working-class Americans which was the culture in which I grew up.

> Me or Uncle CC? Everyone called him CC, his real name was Clarence Cecil Short. I'm blacker because I left America and never came back. CC is less black. After touring the

world in the merchant navy he came back. Inherited grandma Short's house – did it up and sold it, then bought two more houses. Eventually he bought the whole town of South Pekin, Illinois. He was a real estate man, a slum landlord during the depression. He owned two whore houses and a herd of rent boys. During his time in the Merchant Navy, he collected tattoos all over his body even his penis, but you can only see the design when it's erect – I won't go into detail. He was buried 15 years ago with a Swiss bank account number tattooed somewhere on his body – so the rumour goes. My mother employed a detective to try and access the account and get the money. He was probably worth millions.

I started turning black when I failed everything at school. But maybe I'm blacker than CC because I fought for the voting rights of Afro-Americans, civil liberties for Chicanos, better pay for Mexican migrant workers in California, and crosses were burned on my lawn in Bakersfield after I infiltrated the John Birch Society (the western equivalent of the Klu Klux Klan); and because I was convicted of treason and given a five year prison sentence and a $10,000 fine for helping people desert from the army, finding them safe homes in Europe. I was living in Paris at the time – 1967 – at the height of the Vietnam war, the peace group was based at Shakespeare & Son on the Left Bank where we printed anti-war flyers and posters. And because I never went to prison and never paid up. Instead, an English woman agreed to marry me which prevented the US government from extraditing me. Because I burned my passport. Because I burned the American flag. Over a 12 year period I became really black or maybe red in the eyes of the FBI who visited my parents every six months. And because I've never had a proper job. Because I've been divorced twice. And blacker now because I'm living with a German woman with a Sanskrit name and have a British passport.

But when we visited Uncle CC in South Pekin in 1949, he took me and my sister (she's the white sheep, a certified public accountant) to a big department store like Macy's and he said 'ya can have anything ya want.' He was my hero then and my horse when I was geared up in my Roy Rogers cowboy suit, hat and spurs – the very suit I wore when I started thieving at Dick's Supermarket on the corner 4th and Orchard in San Jose. I never got caught but I slowly turned black from inside out.

(Butler 2008, preface)

Since this piece was published, it has generated an enormous amount of comment from close friends and family. My first wife, the English woman, was upset because there was so little about her and the matter-of-fact tone made her feel unloved. So she sent me copies of letters I had written at the time, her own diary entries about the circumstances leading up to our marriage. What became apparent is how two people's shared life experience can be remembered completely differently and even still be different when recorded at the time. I thought she 'offered' to marry me because I was threatened with a prison sentence. She thought I had asked and she 'agreed'. At her request I changed that one word in the above text. And the writing, I believe, has led to a better understanding between us.

People on My Bus *Francesca Creffield*

I have discovered that I am made up of numerous different personalities. There are some I like and many I don't, but to deny any of them is to live an inauthentic life, a life of struggle and resistance under a cloud of fear that there is something very wrong with me which one day would be exposed.

Writing has always helped me express myself but a year ago I faced debilitating writer's block. It wasn't just my writing that felt blocked, I felt frozen in my life, unable to move forwards. I was meant to be self-employed as a writer and workshop facilitator but even writing an email seemed like an enormous effort.

I did a writing exercise taken from Debbie Ford's *The Dark Side of the Light Chasers* (1998). The exercise was to imagine yourself on a bus. Everyone on the bus is an aspect of your psyche, a sub-personality. Your task is to meet and speak with every one of these people, no matter how unsavoury they may appear to be. Ford says that this is one situation where you do well to expect the worst because these people often represent deeply repressed parts of our personalities. You name them, describe them and then begin a dialogue with them.

> The voices of your unembraced qualities when allowed into your consciousness, will bring you back to balance and harmony with your natural rhythms.
>
> (Ford 1998, p.92)

Ford suggests getting off the bus with each person individually. Sit down next to them and ask what trait they represent along with a name. If you don't hear a name give that person one. Notice how they are dressed, how they smell. Notice their mood and body language. Ask, 'What is your gift to me?' and when they have answered ask, 'What do you need to be whole?' or, 'What do you need to integrate into my psyche?' After you have heard every answer ask, 'Is there anything else you need to say to me?' When you are finished make sure you acknowledge this person and walk them back to the bus.

Ford suggests that all this is done in the form of visualisation. You then open your eyes and write down the message you received from your sub-personality before writing for ten minutes in your journal about your experience. I personally found it easier to write it all from beginning to end. I would notice someone on the bus, sometimes because they have a big personality, sometimes because they are very quiet or hiding. Ford says that the ones we feel the most resistant to often have the greatest gift for us and there were some I felt genuinely revolted by, but I spoke with them too. It was an amazing experience and really helped me see why I was so blocked in certain areas of my life.

What helped with my lack of motivation for work was meeting Laura on my bus:

> **Lazy Laura** – eats sweets, takes no exercise, has no ambition or enthusiasm. Her favourite phrase is 'I can't be bothered.' Everything is too much for Laura, even a simple task like cleaning the bin exhausts her. She is slothful, boring and uninteresting. Never reads a book or learns anything, she is a mental loafer. FAT and LAZY, no passion for anything.
> *What is your gift to me Laura?*
> Well I am only like this because you made me. I am here to tell you to rest and treat yourself nicely sometimes, have

some chocolate, put your feet up, celebrate your sobriety, your achievement. My behaviour is a direct result of your constant moaning and nagging, you start first thing in the morning and go on and on until bedtime. There is absolutely no point in doing anything because YOU WILL NEVER BE SATISFIED NO MATTER WHAT I DO. There is no bloody point because even when I have worked hard and sit down to have a break you have a go at me. If I read a book you say it is the wrong book, you view everything fun as a waste of time but never tell me what isn't a waste of time. You need to learn to chill out, get some balance between work and play, encourage me when I do want to do something like read a book or exercise instead of going straight into your controlling, criticising ways. I am not boring and uninteresting just sick and tired of never getting any encouragement or enthusiasm from you.

Every time I sat down to do more of this exercise, words came tumbling onto the page almost as though the sub-personalities were desperate for their chance to speak. It is an ongoing process that I still continue today and I have discovered that it is not just negative aspects of ourselves that can be uncovered. I found many sub-personalities who represented denied talents and positive traits that I really wasn't embracing in my life and work.

Amongst others I have met Spiteful Susan who held the gift of resourcefulness, Busty Bertha, a tarty character who encouraged me to embrace my sexuality and womanhood and not see it as shallow and cheap. There is a woman who I haven't built up the courage to approach yet. She is self-assured and perfectly composed with a warm energy. I am nervous of her because she appears to need nothing. Someone suggested that maybe she is my future – what a lovely thought. Before I can meet with her there are a lot of others still clamouring for my attention.

Every time I read the words that have come from this exercise I feel freer, more productive and a genuine fondness for my inner characters. The pieces of dialogue or descriptions themselves are not something I would necessarily use as material for creative work but embarking on this journey to embrace my shadow has made my other work less self-conscious. I am no longer so fearful of exposure, I have nothing to hide.

Midnight Robber *Dominique De-Light*

Before I was a writer I was a carnival artist. I spent my days (and many nights) carving cane, bending wire, sewing sequins, creating costumes over 20 feet high. I lived in Trinidad, home to the West Indian carnival. I was English but it was this other island, four and half thousand miles away, at the tail end of the Caribbean chain that felt like home. The creativity, the culture, the carnival, was what I lived for. As a white Yorkshire woman, I yearned to learn more so I read anything I could lay my hands on – and discovered as a result some of the best writers of the English language: V.S. Naipaul, Derek Walcott, Earl Lovelace, Samuel Selvon and Shani Mootoo. The writing and language that surrounded me was inspiring. Though I didn't realise it at the time the writer inside me was born: the midwife was culture shock, isolation and self-discovery. Surrounded solely by Trinidadian friends in the days before email my reactions to a foreign culture exploded onto the page in diaries and notebooks, for the time being seen by no one but myself.

Constantly exposed to music in the street, on buses and taxis, the rhythms of the land entered my blood: calypso, soca, the steel drum, chutney – the island was known for its musical invention. I fell in love with its latest permutation, rapso – rap with politically conscious lyrics, and a man who was to become one of the island's leading rapso artistes.

I loved making costumes representing the transience of life but when I wanted my thoughts to have permanence I used the written word. When my relationship imploded, when the rose-coloured glasses fell aside and the island of beauty, creativity and culture revealed a darker side of machismo, poverty and hate, I reached for my pen and a traditional carnival character. The Midnight Robber, dressed in black cape and large hat decorated with skulls, is known for his bombastic speech, his critical words of those in power and his revelations of hypocrisy; a modern-day equivalent of the African griot. In the true tradition of rap battles, I took one of my lover's songs, 'Talk your talk you mocking pretender' whose lyrics lambasted the government – for failure to do what they promised and their hypocritical morals and wrote a song about my lover's hypocrisy and the anger I felt.

Midnight Robber (an extract)
This midnight robber coming down,
She fast, she wicked, she from outta town.
She's come to sting yuh like a swarm of b-e-e-s,
Accent's strange, 'cause she's from Leeds.
This midnight robber come with a dagger,
Ripping down walls of pretence, 'cause she madder,
Than any midnight robbers in town,
The message clear, simple, direct,
Don't mess with my head, or you'll be next.
'Cause I the baddest midnight robber from Leeds.

She exposing, mocking pretenders.
Who ain't dead badly wounded
And this robber's heart is bleeding
Slashed by distrust and despair,
Which is why she raps this year,
Bow not to ignorance, peer pressure nor fear.
It doesn't matter where you are,
Everybody wants to be a star.
Playing dead to catch corbeaux alive,*
Cause the soul to die inside.

Oh yes she mad, really mad, mad, mad.
If accepting things is your normality
I refuse to accept your reality
Reject a world with rich and poor.
Beggars knocking at my door.
I want a world of equality,
People acting honestly,
Till the fight is won,
I causing trouble for everyone
'Cause I mad, I bad, I crazy you see,
'Cause I the midnight robber from Leeds.

(*'Playing dead to catch corbeaux alive' is a common Trinidadian saying, meaning you'll get what you want by pretending to be something you're not.)

By writing as the Midnight Robber I could claim a confidence I didn't feel. By using rapso I could express myself more powerfully. I have found this exercise a useful tool, both for self-expression and when working in therapeutic settings. I choose a folklore myth, a fictional character, whether from book, film or TV and express my emotions through their eyes.

For instance, I choose a favourite soap character: Bett Lynch from Coronation Street. I outline my problems and have her respond to them. I might even write her a reply. This gives the problem distance. It enables me to leap into another personality, gaining a new perspective. A solution may be found, humour may be discovered where there was none before.

> 'But Bett how can toilet shaped earrings improve my love life?'
> 'They're a talking point duck, no man can resist them!'

This exercise has honed my character writing skills, helped me explore points of view, enabled me to express feelings long bottled up. For example, I find it difficult to voice anger but when I write as the Incredible Hulk, it floods out. Using another voice gives me permission to express things I would not normally say. Just like carnival – where costumes are donned to play another character for the day – as a writer words are my costume – creating voices I never knew I had. Just as reading can take you to different worlds, so can pen and paper; writing, along with reading, is my escape.

Usually I choose characters I can relate to, those that not only tell my story but contextualise it in history and politics. For whether we are griots, story tellers, writers or rap artists we all have a message we want to get out there. And as for my Midnight Robber? Well, I had performed another song at a rapso event the year before and was asked to appear at a Women in Rapso concert but I was flying back to England that day. The Midnight Robber was performed to its intended audience – my ex – a few days before I boarded the plane. I got the response I was looking for, a sheepish, 'dat good gyal,' and isn't that what we all want? To be listened to. To be understood. To be heard.

Writing as a Process of Coming-to-Knowing *Rosie Alexander*

There are times in my life when I feel like I lose touch with myself, when I start to have unsettling dreams, feel emotional for no particular reason or feel generally confused. It is at these times that I know that there is something unconscious that I need to process. And I find that writing is the perfect medium for me to come to understand my own thoughts and feelings.

Recently I moved from Cornwall (where I had grown up) to Orkney, in the far north of Scotland. It was a good move and a challenge but also an adventure. However a few weeks after moving I still felt unsettled and I knew that I needed to try and sort out my thoughts. So I sat down to write.

I started in my usual way, setting myself the task of writing rapidly for ten minutes, in a style suggested by Dorothea Brande (amongst others) as a way to free creativity – to write 'rapidly and uncritically', write 'any words at all which are not nonsense', to write 'until you feel that you have utterly written yourself out' (1996, p.66). As the first line can be the most difficult I started by expressing my intention: 'So I feel a lot calmer today than I did yesterday, and I want to process some of my thoughts and feelings about the move…' and then I just wrote.

I wrote rapidly, and for the first few pages I had a nagging thought that 'nothing good would come of this', but that was OK, because my intention was purely to write, and to keep writing for at least ten minutes. So I continued, and in amongst the lines of 'I don't know what to write now…' and 'the ten minutes must be almost up…' I was aware that I was spontaneously using images and ideas that were curious to me. I didn't let this interrupt my flow, but continued to write, knowing that there'd be time later to go back through my work. I kept writing until I reached a point where I felt 'written out', felt that I had written myself into some kind of understanding. In this case this came with the following paragraph:

> I've been living in that existential way (contemplating 'big' questions, like the meaning of life). I've been thinking of death and about these partings which prefigure death. They say it is like heaven here, and mostly in that way that it is so

far and that you are all gone. And there is just me, the sky, the
seals the sea. It's a simple life and I'm attached to the rocks
and the sky. But you can feel the edges of the rocks, they are
less confusing than people. And I know that my thoughts are
my own, that this is me.

This paragraph held exactly the right tone for me, and it also held the
line 'I've been living in that existential way' which intrigued me. I then
went back through my prose and picked out other interesting lines and
images. This gave me plenty of material to play with, plenty of images
to extend, and taking the line 'I've been living in that existential way' as
my starting point, I wrote this poem:

The leaving

I've taken to living in an existential way
I've shed the many skins of my past
I've broken all the knitted strands
of my life and walked away to leave behind
only some papers in an attic, some rubbish
buried in the ground, some clothes
hanging in someone else's closet

And the dust of myself that I gathered
so carefully before has blown with a gust
out amongst the world. My life has shrunk
to what I can carry in the boot of one car,
and the contents of my half empty bookshelves,
are tokens of lives once lived, pieces
of a jigsaw that will never be completed.

But there is a newness in this place.
There is an honesty in all this absence.
The cold northern air sharpens the edges
of things – sharpens the edges of me
So that the rhythms of my life are only mine
lying side by side with the flowing tide
and the steady wind that makes me work to stand

Around me the curlew's dipping cry
draws attention to its solitary ways,
the seal who's been in the bay this past hour
plays like a child, tipping his head back,
nose in the air, to let the water lap along his throat,
And in the sand of the beach each curling spoil
heap shows a separate worm working away

And sitting on this rough banded stone
watching the sea rock through the weeds
I know that no matter how hard I try to explain
down a phone line, in an email or letter no one
can understand what it is to be this alone and this free
to feel myself shifting like the sands in the bay,
Now that I've taken to living in this existential way.

The images of the air sharpening the edges, the seal, struggling to explain over the telephone, the rhythms of the tide, the half-empty bookshelves, the dust of myself – all of these were in my original prose. However, putting them all together into a poetic form helped to contain them and give them structure. The structure also gave some narrative form to my thoughts – starting with an acknowledgement of the grief and loss, the poem offers its own solution in following the rhythms of nature. The movement of the whole poem is towards a calmness. And I have found in the subsequent months that the line about feeling 'myself shifting like the sands in the bay' has stayed with me, like a kind of affirmation, that I have turned over and over in my mind, conveying with it a feeling of calmness and of a purposeful process – a feeling that was so missing when I first sat down to write.

Writing Inspired *Sue Glover Frykman*

Our 'nine senses' were the starting point of a writing exercise in which I asked those taking part in the writing retreat to think about their external senses of sound, smell, taste, sight and touch and the inner senses of pain, balance, thirst and hunger. Before playing Vivaldi's 'Spring', I gave the instructions that when the music had finished group members were to go outside into the grounds or woods around the house, find somewhere to sit, quietly soak up the surroundings and, using all their nine senses, write down whatever came into their heads continuously for 20 to 30 minutes. I did the exercise too, and this is part of the result (unedited):

> I follow the warming alleys of the sun until they lead me to the resting place – a small grassy hummock in the midst of the wood, bathed in a pool of sunlight. For the moment this is my space and my world. But I am not alone. Tinkling, zinging, tutting, burring, zithering sounds pervade my ears. They interrupt each other. Their cadences merge and flow and harmonise as did Vivaldi's impression of Spring. A slight breeze brushes my nose. I feel its cooling breath on my skin until the sun pushes it away.
>
> A gossamer web shimmers before my eyes. How delicate it is – and yet strong enough to trap and ensnare its creator's dinner. A bumble bee circles me, probably wondering who the intruder is. I am inspected a number of times by this hovering being… Bumble bee lands on my shoes and sniffs around. My trouser bottoms appear to have a curious fascination. I must be a very strange lump indeed. Not only that – I've invaded its world. Am I friend, or foe?
>
> That's not a bad question…bee isn't yet convinced that I mean no harm. The circling, droning inspections continue, each one longer in duration. Who is the pest, I catch myself wondering? My innocent intention was to find a quiet spot and write. Aren't bees noisy? I hadn't realised that before.
>
> My strategy is to sit it out and see what happens next. … Nothing! The buzzing stops – abruptly – and the birdsong flows through to my ears once again. How strange, I muse. The bee left me alone as soon as I'd written down my action strategy. Did it read my thoughts, or my words? A pigeon croaks out its deep-throated presence… I wish I understood pigeon…

At the time the piece meant little to me other than writing down what I heard, saw and inwardly felt in an observant, playful and spontaneous way; enjoying the experience of sitting quietly in the wood and imagining myself connected with whatever lived and moved within it. Reflecting on this piece now, 17 months later, leads to three valuable insights. The first is that as a professional translator living and working in Sweden I easily allow my creative writing talents to be cramped in the daily round of transforming other people's words into something worthy of publication in academic journals. Here, in the open air, I was able to play and spontaneously yet mindfully express something of what I felt to be important at the time.

The second insight is that I am deeply connected to Mother Earth and have a personal relationship with her. This is perhaps not surprising considering that I'm a passionate gardener and live in the country. In this piece I even establish some kind of relationship with the bee (albeit one-sided). When I developed this piece further, I dialogued with the bee, wrote from the bee's point of view and explored its inquisitiveness; I included the pigeon's perspective, that of the sun, and the grassy hummock on which I was sitting.

It was this kind of playfulness that first attracted me to Judy Clinton's 'Writing the Spirit' workshops. During that retreat weekend I became hooked on the reflective yet spontaneous way of writing that Judy was promoting. In fact, I was so impressed and inspired that I wrote about the process and illustrated it with some of the playful pieces flowing through me (Glover Frykman 2007).

When Danish Quakers heard about the booklet they invited me to lead a writing retreat. Calling the weekend 'Writing Inspired', I followed the structure of Judy's workshops: warm up by writing non-stop for six minutes about anything that pops into your head and, after a period of reflection, follow this with a longer period of spontaneous writing. My retreat workshop deviated from this pattern in one respect. I used different pieces of music as opening inspiration and closing reflection at each session – alternating between the haunting tones of Norwegian composer, Jan Garbarek and Vivaldi's *Four Seasons*.

During the retreat I learned that music facilitates the exploration of different emotions. Interestingly, anger manifested itself after listening to Jan Garbarek's 'Its Name Is Secret Road' as a prelude to a six-minute spontaneous writing exercise. This music is one minute and 43 seconds of what can only be described as flute-simulated greenshanks and curlews calling across the Caithness tundra. Those haunting sounds reminded me of the fragility of the landscape and the part that greed plays in its destruction, and led me to write about the anger I experienced when Caithness was ravaged by rich people planting non-native conifer trees as a tax dodge and the subsequent eradication of nesting birds.

The third, and perhaps most revealing, insight is the notable absence of smell, taste, touch (tactile), thirst and hunger, which could reflect that most of the time I am only half alive – or half dead – to my senses. This observation is sufficient reason to try the exercise again, this time consciously focusing on all the nine senses. Or why not write nine pieces, each focusing on one sense? A multitude of inspiring possibilities await exploration.

AlphaWrites: 26 Days to Transformation *Kathleen Adams*

I've been a member of an online writing community for 13 years. In spite of geographic distance, we consider each other dear and trusted friends. We are always striving in our collective journey to take our writing deeper.

One day, someone in our group said, 'Let's all spend a month writing every day and posting what we write to this list. No restrictions, no expectations – just write something every day for a month!' Another said, 'I'm going to use the alphabet to structure my writing. Each day I'll choose a word that starts with the next letter of the alphabet, and that will be my theme.' I was greatly interested in that approach, because for nearly 20 years I have used AlphaPoems with my clients and students. An AlphaPoem is a poetic device in which each successive line of the poem starts with the next letter of the alphabet, or of a predetermined word or phrase written vertically down the page. I wrote an essay about AlphaPoems for *Writing Works* (Bolton *et al.* 2006, p.46).

By the time my friend was a third of the way through the alphabet, I could see the dramatic impact of her daily essays. She was layering down to the core of the life issue she had identified in her very first write. Midway through the month I abandoned my own writing project and started AlphaWrites.

I chose the theme of health management. In 2007 I was diagnosed with diabetes. I had made substantial lifestyle adjustments, sufficient to stop the progression of the disease, but I was stalled. Without taking my lifestyle changes to the next level, I knew I would not be able to manage the condition for my optimum health and well-being. Yet I seemed to have a deep pocket of resistance, and I didn't know how to transcend it.

My awakening began with my very first write, which, in fact, came out of a 3:00 a.m. bout with insomnia. 'A is for Awake,' I began, and wrote:

> ... In my work with clients I am always alert for the times when they are making authentic attempts toward genuine change but nothing really changes, despite their best efforts. That is always a signal to me that there is something going on beneath the surface, past the obvious, and we start to gently peel away the layers. That's what I want to do for myself. ... There is something going on here and I don't know what it is. What I want in this 26-day process is to find out what is driving my inability to simply do the things I want to do for my own health. ... Diabetes was a wake-up call, but it didn't create an awakening. So this is where I begin. I begin with the Awakening and I humbly surrender to where it may lead me as I write my way through the layers.

Each morning I sat down at my computer, fingers poised on the keyboard, waiting to catch the word that would deepen my exploration. B was for Baffled (Baffled is how I feel about my diabetes management. It's a complex and confusing disease, sneaky and untrustworthy. I try to give it what it wants and it sabotages me...). Through the early part of the alphabet I plunged to dark places. I wrote a convoluted exploration of my Commitments, a raw and aching essay on how Food and Desire are closely connected, a ramble about my conflicted relationship with Exercise, and a rant on Fear. Inevitably, the word selected itself. The essays tumbled forth in a torrent of writing, usually taking about 45 minutes and averaging about 1000 words.

On the 7th day, G was for Gratitude. Despite my conflicted relationship with it most of my life, my body is amazing, and I am in awe of what it does for me, I began, and out flowed an homage of devotion and respect:

> When I listen to my body and give it respect and attention...,
> it shares its wisdom with me. When I ignore it or get superior

and tell it that I know best, it simply withdraws into silence and, without any judgment whatsoever, allows me to override it. … My body has grace, wisdom, strength, flexibility, innate knowledge, balance, miraculous functioning, patience, steadiness, stamina, faithfulness, love for me and an unending forgiveness that I don't deserve. … I commit, here and now, to release the bafflement, stay awakened to its profound wisdom, and listen deeply to its whispers of guidance.

Through the alphabet I roamed. There were plunges back into the pits of darkness, and climbs back up into the light, but by S – for Setbacks and Starting Over – I was moving forward with momentum and determination. My Z write – Zygote – was a mere 100 words and summarised the journey triumphantly:

Although the dictionary definitions are still too scientific and complicated for my liberal arts brain, I think I understand zygote to be the single cell formed by fertilization of the egg by the sperm. Which means it is The Beginning, the union of yin and yang, the point from which all else develops and grows. And so, in this ending, I begin.

Since I completed the AlphaWrites, I have made quietly dramatic changes in lifestyle that are having measurable positive effects on the management of my diabetes. I am significantly less baffled, substantially more committed, almost free from fear, and I live in a state of near-constant gratitude and appreciation. As I wrote in T, for Transcendence:

A lifetime of struggle and suffering, deeply influenced by a 26-day pattern of writing? It seems absurd in its simplicity, and yet what if it is true? Is this method indeed a portal into actual transcendence of lifelong behavioral and belief patterns? We shall see. Meanwhile, I hold the vision of transcendence.

Writing Loops *Briony Goffin*

On my bookshelves I have several beautiful hard-backed notebooks – embroidered covers, heavy-quality paper, ribbon markers, each with the first four or five pages torn out. I would collect them from fancy gifts shops, seduced by their clean white interior and the possibilities this space held. I have carried them around in my handbag, in my pockets, positioned them on my bedside table, packed them in my holiday luggage. Evidence of my desire to write – to write for myself – could be traced all over my world.

Yet, in those moments when I 'set myself up' to write, what came out on the page felt remote. It didn't sound like me. But what did I sound like to myself? I knew what my voice sounded like when I was amidst my family, my friends, or my work clients. Each variation had its own familiar nuances, expressive patterns and frames of reference, and came readily to me. But when I began writing for myself – explicitly identifying myself as the only audience – I noticed I was still attempting to hone my voice for all the different people in my life. In my eagerness to fulfil their multiple expectations of me, I adopted a voice that spoke out into a kind of limbo-place – and invariably it sounded like nothing.

The experience had become no more than a fraught performance. In my disillusionment, the pages of my beautiful notebooks were torn out.

The idea of 'writing loops' was borne out of a faith that I would discover a more personal or private voice if I persisted, and that an authentic voice wasn't necessarily the one that was most accessible. It may require drawing out.

I began by choosing a small and simple moment to write about – lying in bed and listening to fireworks. I admit, ashamedly, that I began writing with the desire to sound 'literary'. Invariably, the first few lines sounded pretentious and detached. I registered my instinct to give up. But, I went back to the beginning and re-wrote it. This time I imagined describing the scene to friends, the idea being that this might facilitate a more 'familiar' tone. I recognised my wish to sound full of spark, wit and self-mockery, as if writing my own column for a weekend supplement. The voice felt warmer but some of the content seemed superficial. I returned again to my opening line, this time acknowledging the more sober nature of the scene, picking up details that referred to a sense of aloneness.

This repetitive action, or looping back on myself, allowed for new information to be integrated into the image and for the scene to grow in complexity. Each loop presented the possibility of re-creating the picture from another angle or from an alternative voice. Or, I might fine-tune the line that came before so that the language more accurately evoked the emotional content of the scene. Once I felt I had got closer to the heart of each moment, I could move on to the next series of lines. Whenever the language felt out of kilter with the experience I would continue the looping process.

The momentum of this method allowed for the accumulation of courage. With every repetition I was able to stay longer in that moment and look more closely at the scene. My expression, too, became braver as I began to say things with fewer words and less hesitation. This process felt not dissimilar to the practice of systematic desensitisation – the incremental exposure to a feared scenario. For me, I feared seeing the presence of sadness or loss in the scene.

On reading the writing back, I noticed its repetitious quality sounded canon-like in its expression, with a phrase in one part being successively taken up by one or more other parts. This choral analogy felt revelatory. Instead of rejecting the multiplicity of my voice it helped me see that several voices overlapping, all chiming together, created a sense of layeredness. And that this layeredness referred to the possibility of several different emotions, as embodied by the different voices, as able to co-exist in any one moment.

This writing technique has given the different parts of myself the space to be heard – including those voices I might otherwise dismiss as sounding too trivial, serious or perverse. Indeed, it regards every voice as having something of significance to say. It is this democracy that allows me to be most of what I am in any one moment, even if it's contradictory. So instead of misdirecting energy in the inhibition of 'inappropriate' voices, I am freed up to experience myself in the round.

This writing technique is also characterised by its patience. It accepts that resistances exist and doesn't deride me for possessing them. Instead, the looping action dissolves my resistance, helping me depict my world, and myself in that world, with greater clarity. And, at every juncture, I am in control of the pace. This has given me the courage to take on any subject, however big, abstract, or emotionally complex. All I have to do is start somewhere, in the knowledge that the first voice isn't definitive, and let all sorts of additional voices surface. The looping action will make space for one clear, more resonant voice to sing out through all the others.

Most of the notebooks on my bookshelves are now filled and ringing with multiple parts. The most recent books however are defined by a more singular expression. This doesn't mean that I've siphoned off particular voices, quite the opposite, by maintaining a practice I've been able to integrate them into one voice – a singular note but one that is characterised by its own spectrum of harmonics. This is the voice that seems to come through at the moment, in a clear loop from myself to myself, and it feels familiar.

Here is an unedited extract from an old notebook:

> ... Last night I lay in bed listening to fireworks. Last night I lay on the edge of my bed with my arm stretched over the empty side, listening to fireworks. This is what it might sound like to be at war, to be at war on the edge of my bed with my arm stretched over the empty space. My heart beating into the mattress, imagining the crowds by the fountains, faces turned upwards to the sky. Last night I watched the fireworks from my window with the lights off, at the window in my nightie, at the window in my nightie hoping the neighbours won't see me. It's still early and I'm in the dark watching the fireworks from my bedroom window, I hope my neighbours don't see me as they gather on their doorsteps. The seagulls have risen, the seagulls are flapping above the stadium, the underside of their wings lit up. The couple from downstairs come home, and then leave again. My telephone rings. My telephone rings, I move away from the window until it stops. Last night I heard the fireworks...

Finding Your Racket Voice *Sandy Hutchinson Nunns*

As a therapist I use writing, my own and clients', to look for an extra dimension of meaning. Often the analysis of one piece leads to the writing of another in a never-ending unfolding of self-knowledge.

I find that when rereading my writing, I can see another Self there that I had been unaware of at the time of writing. Talking to a fellow writer about this phenomenon, her response was to ask how I recognised this other Self, which set me thinking.

My mind went to a poem I'd written in response to a colleague's request for me to 'look at equal opportunities' (meaning, 'investigate disabled access issues for a conference we were organising') 'because I had arthritis'. I had been so angry at this I stopped in a lay-by on the way home from the meeting to write out my feelings; I literally could not contain them, even to get home.

Equal Opportunities
You ask about my arthritic joints
About access and how it feels
About separateness and all that stuff

When I am a woman in a man's world
A Northerner in the South
Short amongst the tall people
Fat amongst the fashionably slender
Working class amongst the middle
Intelligent amongst the mediocre
Feminist amongst the patriarchal
A Goddess woman amongst the Father's children
Twisted-faced amongst the beautiful
Wombless amongst the fertile
Howling my rage at children stolen
Motherless, and that her choice.

What comparatively minor things
These climbing stairs and swollen places
Quite obvious the remedy you'd think.
But the other stuff,
The hidden secrets,
These too are there to see.
You've got two eyes, a brain, imagination,
Bugger off and sort it out then
I've got a life to live.

That was several years ago and I'd set the poem aside, not knowing what to make of it all. Why had I responded to an honest request in such a vehement way? I put the piece in my file, but occasionally it would pop into my head or come up in a conversation and so the words stayed alive for me.

Years later, I attended a workshop given by an eminent Transactional Analyst. (See Woollams and Brown 1978, for an account of TA.) She introduced some theory that I thought I knew well in a new context, and suddenly I knew what the poem was about. I had heard my Racket Voice.

Erskine and Zalcman (1979) described a model of interlocking and self-reinforcing beliefs and behaviours that they called the Racket System. The model is a way of analysing repressed needs and feelings which Transactional Analysis calls 'script' (Erskine and Zalcman 1979, pp.51–59).

There are three major components to this model, each part reinforcing the other to set up a dynamic system. The part that caught my attention was when the presenter wrote on her flip chart: 'Beliefs about: Self, Others, the Environment (the world is…).'

If I approach my poem using Racket Theory, what does my Self who is this poem's narrator believe about 'self, others and the environment?' How does that Self demonstrate those beliefs?

I concluded that: my view of myself is of someone overlooked, not seen: my view of others is that they reject certain aspects of me: my view of the environment is that it requires me to adapt to it, not allowing me to be myself.

I realised that the narrator of the poem (that is, me!) was repressing feelings of pain, of isolation and sadness at not being like others and instead was only expressing the anger I was experiencing: a feeling that was allowed in my childhood. The anger is real, but it is not the whole story; hence my feeling that there was a problem at the time of writing. I knew how to be angry and had yet to learn how to express the sadness and isolation.

My narrator Self is reporting the internal experience reinforced by old memories in the poem about myself as outsider, others as persecutory and the environment as hostile. What I now see is that the anger the narrator feels is focused on the injustice she experiences, that she has not been seen as a whole person, that is, she has not been met with 'equal opportunity'.

I now have more information about this person, this Self who wrote in the lay-by. I realise that there is truth in the poem but it's not the whole picture. Examining what this Self believes about 'self, others and the world', and how these beliefs are maintained, is a way of capturing information that wasn't obvious to the original narrator Self.

The difference now is that I see my part in maintaining this. Yes, things happened in my life, but I was railing against the external injustice. This was a passive position; external events are not something I have control over.

The shift in my understanding of what I was writing about is that I now realise the control I have is internal – I can passively accept external definitions of who I am, or I can stand in my own truth.

I already had the information I needed when I wrote the poem, but it took years for me to put all the pieces together. By analysing the poem in terms of the Racket System, I could see the difference between who I was and who I am. I am 'living my life' but I don't need others to 'bugger off' anymore.

Although this technique is a *post hoc* analysis, now I see how to use the Racket System in this way, I am able to apply it to what I am writing at the time. I find it a clear lens with which to look at my own and my clients' unconscious process as revealed in the written word.

CHAPTER 4

Writing the Body

Edited by Victoria Field

Our bodies are often mysterious to us and can be a source of both pleasure and pain. We can experience our bodies as what we essentially 'are' and yet, sometimes, they can feel distinctly 'other'. Most of the time, we ignore much of what our bodies do but when we suffer illness, accident or deliberate harm, it can be difficult to think of anything else. At these times, writing can be a way of engaging, understanding and even taking control.

Beverly Kirkhart came to writing through the encouragement of her oncology nurse and found that in spite of initial resistance, daily journaling helped clear her mind of negative thoughts. Jane Pace shows how simple journal-writing prompts enabled her to process complex feelings around her long ago rape. Her writing helped her to 'hear herself' at a difficult time.

Sue Ashby describes a specific writing exercise designed to focus awareness on a part of the body and discovers how this can act as a wake-up call not to ignore distress. Miriam Halahmy shows how list-writing, among other journal techniques, helped her cope with chronic pain and a serious operation.

Writing can also help at times of others' illness. Bryony Doran describes how she gradually created a poem based on traumatic memories of her son's facial surgery. Jay Carpenter writes of his experience observing patients with eating disorders. Claire Willis, who facilitates writing for people with cancer, explores how her feelings around this work and her own concerns about 'legacy' were processed through journal exercises.

Finding Beauty in an Ugly Situation *Beverly Kirkhart*

You want me to do what? Write my thoughts down in a journal? I hate to write. I'm dyslexic and besides I don't know what to put on paper. How do I feel, you ask? I don't know. I'm overwhelmed with unfamiliar feelings of anger, despair and fear. Why would I ever want to re-read these depressing thoughts? Reading them again will only make me feel worse…and heaven forbid if someone was to read what I wrote.

These were my first thoughts as I resisted the suggestion from my oncology nurse to write in a journal. My healthcare provider strongly believed journaling would help me cope with my deepest feelings that came with my cancer diagnosis.

Today, I'm so grateful for my nurses' encouragement to journal daily. As a result of pouring out my frightening and unfamiliar feelings onto paper I was able to clear my mind from the negative thoughts that were keeping me from believing in myself.

Before cancer, I was living the American dream. I was married to my college sweetheart, and with my husband of 17 years we designed and built our dream house in the foothills of Santa Barbara, CA. I also owned and operated an 18-room inn in Santa Barbara, CA. I loved my life!

But, in 1991, my dream life shattered. I lost my marriage to a divorce. I was forced to file bankruptcy losing my inn, financial security and dream home. As I was facing all these hardships, I remember telling my family: at least I had my health. In October 1993, I was diagnosed with breast cancer. Hearing the word 'cancer' was overwhelming and deeply terrifying. I was told my tumour was aggressive. Suddenly, I was forced to stare death in the face, making major life decisions alone, and a destitute living out of a car. Just getting out of bed each morning and facing another day was extremely difficult, depressing and daunting.

As a result of the culmination of all my tragedies, my life was turned upside down – leaving me helpless, angry, afraid and sad. These feelings were frightening and unfamiliar to me. So rather than face them I buried them. But these disturbing thoughts weren't going away. They showed up in various ways in my life, that I wasn't aware of, such as yelling at my compassionate care-givers, drinking too much while being treated with chemotherapy, or playing out the victim role – 'Why me?'

I soon found myself in a deep depression. I would have stayed in this horrible state if it hadn't been for the loving nudging and persistent suggestions from my oncology nurse to try writing my thoughts on paper. As I sat in the chemo chair my nurse would say, 'Write down one word that describes how you feel right now.' My response to her was, 'I don't know how I feel, maybe overwhelmed.' The next words she spoke changed my life forever, 'Write that word, "overwhelmed", down on this paper.' Following her instructions, I began writing a sentence about feeling overwhelmed. As the pen flowed on the paper so did my thoughts. My words flooded out... 'I'm angry because...I'm scared because...I feel betrayed because...' While the cocktail of drugs was flowing through my body, the pen never left the paper.

After my initial treatment I went straight to a stationery store and I bought my very first journal. This journal became my constant companion and it never left my side. I could write anything and know I wasn't going to be judged or criticised. I found journaling so powerful that I wanted to share this method of coping with other cancer survivors. I took excerpts of my journal and published these entries in my book, *My Healing Companion*, which is now in its fourth edition with 150,000 copies in print.

This book contains the questions and activities which I found to be helpful during my cancer journey. One example, in the chapter 'I want to Be Positive, but I Feel So Negative', invites the reader to 'think of positive benefits that you might never have come to appreciate before your cancer diagnosis'. When I began my cancer journey, I was filled with negativity. I saw my life half-empty not half-full. I did not appreciate anyone or anything in my life. But after I sat down and began to list the things I was so grateful for and why, I slowly began to recognise the beauty in an ugly situation.

My writing helped me articulate my fears, anger, sadness, wants and dreams. From my daily writing I grew to realise that I wasn't a 'cancer victim' but rather an individual with God-given gifts. Journaling helped me to discover my strength and articulate more clearly my feeling which, in turn, helped me to communicate more effectively with my healthcare team and my loving care-givers.

Fifteen years on from my diagnosis, journaling is still an essential part of my daily schedule. Faithfully every morning I curl up in my favourite chair, put on a soft meditation CD, light a candle and begin my journaling adventure. It's an adventure because I never know where my thoughts are going to lead me, or what my inner wisdom will reveal to me on any given day. Sometimes the words float across the page with ease, and at other times I struggle to find one or two words to express myself. But, the adventure is in the experience and excitement of writing whatever comes to my mind, and going wherever my thoughts lead me. When I've reached the end of my writing and I put the pen down, I'm filled with a sense of freedom and joy.

Listening to Body Signals: Triggers from the Past
Jane Pace

One evening, in Denver Colorado, I had just come home from a birthday dinner celebration with friends. As I got out of my car, I noticed once again police helicopters flying over the area. I went in and turned on the TV news. After I learned what had happened I shut down the TV and wrote.

At that time, I was in the process of using Ilene Segalove's (2004) book, *40 Days and 40 Nights: Taking Time Out for Self Discovery, A Guided Journal*. I was on Day 7 and the theme for that day was 'Listen to Your Heart'. Segalove lists several prompts. Two are always specific to the topic and the other choice is a daily prompt using the word *Today…* I started with the prompt: *Today…*

> Today and tonight and yesterday and yester night it is all beginning to haunt me inside. This serial rapist in my neighbourhood taking down women and children. A man who is out of control and is desperately trying to get caught. But he isn't yet. And another one tonight – while I sat home quietly doing nothing as he attacked a woman just across the park…

This just brings up my very long ago rape. It's visceral and makes my skin crawl. But this is not just an isolated rape. This is one man raping women and children in my neighbourhood. My experience is so buried I forget what it feels like for these 4 women and 2 children. I forget how much shock I was in and how numb. I walked around disconnected from myself and scared, scared, scared. I stayed with friends, talked to my professors, delayed my graduate papers, found a new place to live, went home to stay with my parents for a couple of weeks. It was quite devastating to me inside and out. So all ye cops of Denver, Aurora, and the FBI. Go Forth. Get the Sucker and Take Him Down.

He was caught two hours later with one of the victims 150 miles west of Denver. She suffered horrific physical and emotional trauma. Another victim, who was discovered by police in an apartment building, had been beaten severely and repeatedly raped, was taken to hospital. She was found dead of an overdose a few months later.

The next day I attended a rally organised by one of the victims and her friends. I was then on Day 8 of the guided journal and the theme was 'Ask for Guidance'. As usual, there were exercises and two specific journal prompts plus the prompt *Today...*

Today I went to the rally for the Rape Victims. It was interesting to hear the speakers talk and voice things that I most likely needed to hear: particularly that I did not always hear back in that time zone (25 years earlier). 'You are not alone.' 'You did nothing wrong.' 'It wasn't your fault.' and that I was 'courageous.'

I was courageous to withstand the assault, to call the cops, to expose myself to questioning over and over again and to continue with my life. So it turned out to be affirming for me and I hope for others... I am tired today possibly from the week of craziness and fear in the neighbourhood. I have my doors open again and Mimi (my cat) and I have the curtains open and we are quiet in our little selves. I hope others who were victimised come forth for themselves. You are not alone. You did everything right. You survived.

In terms of journal techniques, I mainly used the prompt of 'today' as a springboard and did stream of consciousness writing, also known as 'free-intuitive writing'. These entries clearly tapped into what was disturbing my psyche at the time, even though I had not mentioned it in previous journal entries. Perhaps the day's assignment 'Listen to Your Heart' provided the right context for me to acknowledge the wave of anxiety and sadness that I had been feeling for the past two weeks. I noticed that writing these words diffused my edginess and gave me breathing space. I had found that it had been difficult to speak freely of my fears to friends. The writing provided a safe place for me to hear myself and acknowledge how much this ongoing situation had been impacting me emotionally.

The second day's entry helped me close a long ago gap that I had never recognised. It was very strengthening to me to view myself as courageous in my actions. This was the first time I *thoroughly* acknowledged that quality within me. Indeed, I felt compelled to come home from the rally and reflect on what I heard and put it in writing so I was connected to the meaning of the words and sit with them. For me, this proved more healing than just having them inside my head. I required a place to remember this shift in perception of myself that was more permanent and where I could go to remind myself, when and if needed.

Straight from the Hip *Sue Ashby*

I wrote the poem below in a *Healing Words: Writing the Body* workshop that I was facilitating. Of the six participants present all had some experience of therapeutic writing and were using the workshop for both personal and professional development. This poem came out of the second exercise I set after a six-minute period of free flow writing and a longer piece of writing (15 minutes). In it, I used a technique developed by Fritz Perls to encourage clients to explore body sensations (Passons 1975). Participants were invited to bring to mind an image that represented a good memory of a part of their body coming into contact with one of the elements – earth, air, fire, water.

After the feedback for that exercise I asked participants to close their eyes and allow themselves to scan their bodies externally and internally and identify something not working as effectively as normal. After writing a list of all the things they knew, felt and thought about that part of their body I invited them to use some or all these words and write a poem/story about that part of the body.

Using Kathleen Adams' intervention of Write from Within (Adams 2004, p.88), I devised some questions for participants to consider that might help them get started:

Q: Is it on the left or right side of your body?

Q: If it is one of a pair, might it want to contact the same part on the opposite side of your body?

Q. What might it say or do?

In these sessions I always write alongside the participants and on this occasion I chose to write about my left hip which had been painful for six or seven weeks. I had not sought medical help, just hoped it would go away. But it didn't and was so painful that at times people asked me why I was limping.

For my own piece of writing I used another Gestalt technique (Yontef 1993), allowing the part of my body I'd selected to speak directly to me (Passons 1975). As a psychotherapist (Certified Transactional Analyst: see Woollams and Brown 1978, for an account of TA) and a writer of plays, I had always been interested in Gestalt therapeutic models and strategies. My own therapy over two years had been with two separate Gestalt therapists, dialoguing with people, places, objects and parts of the body in dreams and listening to what they had to tell me. During this period I also worked with a client recovering from a miscarriage, and invited her to use the Gestalt technique of talking as her womb to successful therapeutic effect.

The poem below is the result of using this strategy and was written quickly as the title suggests. It needed little in the way of crafting afterwards.

Straight from the Hip
Hey you, shut up. Stop complaining.
Remember,
I'm a life-long supporter of yours.
Okay so I've got you into trouble a few times
But we've had some fun, haven't we?

Remember how I squiggled and giggled when you were a kid
being tickled?
How I kept your balance as you swayed from side to side
the day you learnt to ride a bike?
How I squirmed and protested, trying to hide when you were
    spanked?

I was a prime mover in your bid to attract men
Saying look at me!
Here I am.
Curvy in a dress
Swaying gently
Salsaing sexily
All woman.

Okay so I'm letting you down at the moment.
Stay cool.
This stiffness will pass.
All I need is some care and attention
A bit of oil to ease the creaks and groans
And I'll recover
You'll get your equilibrium back
Stride again across the fields
Glide along corridors
Arrive gracefully.

All that I've changed, several times, is the title. Now I'm happy with it.

I was surprised at how annoyed with me my hip was, how it attacked me for ignoring it after all it had done for me. The message was clear, direct, unequivocal. It challenged me to stop behaving in this way. 'Give me some care and attention,' my hip ordered me, something I'd neglected to do in the futile hope the pain would go away.

This behaviour of neglecting something that was actually painful was, and can still be, a 'script' issue for me. Eric Berne defined the life script as an unconscious life-plan (Berne 1966). Three things that affect the life script are drivers, identified by Kahler (Kahler and Capers 1974), and injunctions and decisions identified by Bob and Mary Goulding (Goulding and Goulding 1976). The injunction, 'Don't Be Important' (sometimes interpreted as 'Don't Have Needs') and the driver, 'Be

Strong', were early messages from my parents. The latter was issued on my arrival home from hospital, ten days after I was born. Both led to my decisions to be stoic, put on a brave face and not give in to pain. Only by behaving in these ways would I be accepted by my family. There was a price to pay, though. Because my needs in early infancy were neglected, so I grew up neglecting my own needs.

After writing the above poem I had to take notice and behave differently. Because my hip and the pain were important enough for me to acknowledge, I stopped being strong and gave into my need to rest. Within days the pain was gone.

Such a powerful experience needed to be handed on and I always use this exercise in therapeutic writing groups where the focus is on the body.

It has also been important for me to revisit this experience. It reminds me that I need to take notice of my body's aches and pains and act more quickly to seek treatment and rest than I often do.

Dealing with Chronic Pain *Miriam Halahmy*

I have suffered from inherited osteoarthritis for 16 years, since I was 40. I was in denial for a long time, refusing to take anti-inflammatory drugs, insisting on walking way beyond my capacity and in massive pain. As I turned 50, between X-rays, my rheumatologist announced, 'You have advanced osteoarthritis and both your hips need to be replaced.' I burst into tears and he said sharply, 'I haven't got time for this; I have a roomful of patients out there!'

As I walked out of the hospital the fear and anger which welled up inside me threatened to engulf me. Most of all I was terrified of the wound. There was only one place where I could safely express my feelings – in my journal. Only in those pages could I admit my deepest fears, 'My leg will turn to a mess of mushy pulp, I won't be able to ever touch the wound, the scar will be massive, it'll never fade!'

Writing has always been the most important crutch of my life and I have kept journals since childhood. Now faced with the reality of arthritis, chronic pain and two major operations, my journal seemed the only safe place to fully express myself. It was the first thing I packed when I went into hospital, and the first place I turned to when I came round from the anaesthetic, groggy with morphine, my hand wobbling, '…if I write I might feel better, had a wash, must…' Even fragments have their place in journal writing. They demonstrate the powerful need to write things down.

My journal writing manifests itself in many shapes and forms, from poetry, to rants in capital letters. At times I can only write lists, especially during a period of severe pain. If my hands are swollen and tender, the walk to the laptop a step too far, I can usually write a list in my journal.

On days when I feel less than useless I write a list of who I am, 'mother/sister/cousin/good listener…' to boost my self-esteem. Sometimes I list achievements 'walked across living room without stick/ new poem published…' Sometimes my lists are orders shouted to myself on days when the pain is overwhelming and the drugs just slicing off the top layer, 'Get over it! Be satisfied! Stop whining!'

> *List of most loathed reactions: 15 October 2005*
> Someone offering me their arm to lean on, especially if they are older than me!
> People telling me it's good for me to walk, take exercise, swim, etc. when they haven't a clue.
> People telling me if I ate/didn't eat: tomatoes, glucosamine, potatoes, nettles, I wouldn't have arthritis.
> People who tell me if I read this book, listened to that tape, then I wouldn't have arthritis.
> People who don't believe I have arthritis.
> People with arthritis who don't believe I have arthritis.

This was a list I would not have shared with anyone else at the time, especially as some of these comments were from people quite close to me. Writing in my journal helped me to express my anger and frustration. Having written the list and vented my feelings I became stronger at standing up to people when they were being insensitive. The act of writing helped me to assert myself.

Another aspect of journal writing I really value is being able to repeat things as often as I like without annoying anyone. I develop mantras and write them out at the end of my flow of writing, sometimes in capital letters. 'Keep busy, that's the key'/'Manage pain, don't let it manage you'/'BE STRONG'/'DIG DEEP.' Sometimes these mantras are the only way back to positive thinking on my darkest days.

My journal is also the place where I can make a plan when I feel overwhelmed. With a plan I am more in control. Before my first hip replacement, I was haunted by visions of the wound, the surgeon slashing through the layers of muscles, severing arteries and nerves all the way to the bone and then the whizz of the electric saw removing the rotten hip. In my journal I wrote plan after plan, how to manage each day until the operation, each hour and finally each minute, 'breathe, listen to music, visualise your fave beach, breathe, don't think about it, DON'T ARGUE!' The day I went into hospital, clutching my journal, I was in tears. The woman in the next bed was so upset she vomited.

In my journal I can write whatever I need to write, allowing huge mood swings and contradictions which would be frankly dangerous in the real world. Sometimes even my journal doesn't feel safe and I can only write in code. Writing helps me to come to terms with things I can never admit out loud. I can share the extract below because of the time lapse since I wrote it.

8 October 2005: three months to go
Today I went to the shopping mall with my daughter. I was seriously thinking of getting a disabled scooter from shop mobility, but I didn't have the nerve to ask for one. God! I used to run everywhere; people have no idea. I used to climb, abseil, ski, ride, travel all over the world. They say that the replacement will change my life. But what if it doesn't? It won't alter the arthritis in my spine and my lousy right foot which keeps collapsing and landing me on the pavement and my hands which hurt when I type, write, paint, let alone cook, drive, open jars, peel potatoes and never again will I chop parsnip, no way!
I don't want them to take out my hip. It's been there all my life, it belongs to me. But I don't have a choice. I can't walk anymore.

This extract reveals my deepest feelings about my disability and about losing a part of my body. I felt that saying this out loud sounded like whining. Most people gave little thought to the process I was facing. They would say cheerfully, 'Soon be over and then you'll be able to walk again.' Leaning on my journal at this dark time, was as important as the Zimmer frame they gave me on the ward to get to the toilet. The very act of writing down these thoughts helped me to accept the loss of my joints, mourn them and then move on. I love my prostheses now. They look strong and secure on the X-rays and I have learnt to rely on them. And the scars? You'd need a magnifying glass!

Broken Face – A Poem *Bryony Doran*

> Already the windows are freaked with dawn, at last you are sleeping. I watch the houses coming out into the day, your breath misting the mask...

Yes, I did mean to write 'freaked' and not 'streaked'. I was emerging from a very traumatic experience and the jagged lines of the clouds, crisscrossed with contrails, aptly matched the turmoil I felt.

> Strangers, while he has slept, have broken his face

As so often with my writing, the idea for this work was generated in a workshop environment. The first subject chosen was 'Sky'. Sheffield is a place of many hills, and the view across the city was magnificent.

We gave ourselves ten minutes in which to write. I wrote a page of stream-of-consciousness prose. Afterwards we read our work out to the group. I got halfway through my piece and found I had to stop; I had become too emotional to continue. All of the feelings that I had earlier suppressed were exposed on the page.

A month later I came back to examine my work. The images of my experience were still very vivid and, using the prose and the invoked emotions, I wrote it as a poem.

Over the period of the next year I worked on the poem. Most of the alterations were very small. My poetry group made various suggestions, some of which I agreed with such as the suggestion to change the title, originally 'Oxygen', and to have the penultimate line as the last.

Once I have the core of a poem down on paper I transfer it to my laptop. It took me many months to do this, having taken me a long time to feel strong enough to return to it.

Broken Face
Beads of ruby red drain and draw from ballooned cheeks
pool in bottles under the bed
breath mists the mask, a green of sun on pale water
– a horse trough in France, water
cleansed by a ball of ashen clay
a clarity that entranced us both back then
him teetering on tip toe to peer down.

The nurse lifts the mask, the straps, seaweed green,
cut across his mutilated face
'water' I hear his voice
she turns away 'no water'
'he wants water'
she hands me a pack of pink foam lollipops
'you can swab his mouth.'

Lips the colour of conkers, formless as old shoes
I dab, tentative, recall the fear,
the scar of his umbilical cord
gently, so gently I roll the pink lollipop
see it stain to blood, poke deeper
his tongue is livid, bruised to liver,
congealed with blood
he gapes like a fish, his eyes wild,
anger that masks fear, I look away,
place back the pale green of the mask
hide the violent scar.

He gives up,
arcs his head away, back against the white pillows
closes his eyes
iodine stains darken his neck, yellow leaches his cheeks
strangers, while he has slept, have broken his face
and yet, still perfectly placed above each eye
polished as black talons
the exquisite curve of his brow

Two weeks before the inception of this poem, my son had gone into hospital for an operation on his jaw. Although he was 18 at the time, I don't think either of us had realised the seriousness of the operation. I arrived at the hospital to find that he was in the High Dependency Unit and in a terrible state. I wanted to stay with him overnight and when I was told I couldn't, I felt as though I'd betrayed him.

When we were asked to write about 'Sky' in the workshop, I imagined that I'd been allowed to stay with my son overnight and the sky I wrote about was that I might have seen from the windows when it was coming light. In fact, what I had seen was the skyline at dusk the evening my son was moved down into an ordinary ward.

During this period I was so overcome by the level of emotion I was trying to contain that I felt as if I was losing my mind. By writing the poem I was able to realise and expose the emotions I was feeling and felt better able to cope with life and nursing my son.

The poem expresses the many conflicting emotions and feelings I experienced, among them:

> **Confusion:** He had grown away from me and here he was, a boy again and I was experiencing the joy I had felt back then – in the lines: *a horse trough in France, water / ...him teetering on tip toe to peer down*

> **Fear:** For his life – in the lines: *I dab, tentative, recall the fear / the scar of his umbilical cord*

> **Guilt:** That I had allowed him to have the operation: *he gapes like a fish, his eyes wild / anger that masks fear, I look away,*

During his recovery I went on to write a series of poems depicting how my son coped, by great good humour and courage, with having his jaw wired for six weeks, and how I became his translator.

I learned from writing this poem that ultimately I have benefited from the experience. The emotions I felt, although totally overwhelming, taught me a great deal about my own resilience and strengthened my bond with my son and others around me.

I primarily wrote this poem for myself but I have read this poem at several performances and find that it still affects me emotionally.

However, the feedback I received leads me to believe that it has a very powerful effect. I hope that in writing this poem I have also helped and enriched others.

In Watching You I See Myself *Jay Carpenter*

As a member of staff working within an eating disorder service run by the NHS, I would often sit in the hour-long meal support that took place after each meal of the day. Up to ten patients and two members of staff would make up this group. During this time lots of emotions could arise and not just from the previous meal. Sometimes emotions from way back in the past could surface. On some occasions lots of tears flowed but more often than not there was silence, lots of silence. Watching, just watching rendered me frustrated, very frustrated. Can I help? Maybe, but I sit here time after time watching and waiting.

Watching the silence was very important. A rich unspoken dialogue occurs. In the book *Prompted to Write* (Ansari and Field 2007), Caroline Carver asks, 'Can we write about other people's pain? And do we have the right to do so?' I find this question an interesting one. I feel the question is not for me to answer here but it does take me back to the work I mentioned in the above paragraph.

When I have taken part in a creative writing workshop I have sometimes been given a writing prompt, this could be one word or the first line of a poem. In this case, rather than using words as a prompt, I took one of the patients I was already working with and observed them in their process of anxiety. I watched how they were sitting and their facial expression and transformed this into words. Once the first words were committed to paper, I just continued to write, not worrying about spelling or grammar. This technique, usually called freewriting, is one I was taught while studying creative writing with the Open University. (Anderson 2006). I feel that the healing potential of my writing is further enhanced by using traditional pen and paper rather than switching on my laptop. Moving pen across paper allows me a much truer connection to what I am writing and thus the whole process becomes more organic.

The following poem was first written in a single stanza because it was important for me not to block the flow of words that was connecting me to my feeling.

So Full

I sit here tired, my mind's a blank.
My stomach is full, my head full of thoughts.
Darkness shadows my mind.
The stillness, so loud, despair fills the room.
The darkness calls and is pulling me in.
I curl into a ball, cat-like on its rug,
It's safer this way.
Why? Why? Will these thoughts not go away?
They make me tired; I'm feeling so sick of myself.

If only someone knew of my agony and despair,
Oh! Please let these thoughts go from my head.
I'm feeling tired and full.
The agony and pain, when will it ever end?
No sooner does one meal end then another begins.
The ongoing turmoil puts me in a spin,
Deep down I know this is where I'm meant to be.
Thoughts in my head keep fighting with me.
One day my cloud will lift,
And the sun will shine again, again, shine with me.
But just for now this burden I will carry.
And within each step I take my load lightens.
It is only then that I shall truly understand me.

Once my flow had stopped, I then set about going through what I had written and shaping the words into stanzas. Once this was complete I then left it for a week or so before reading back what I had caught in that moment. Sometimes when spontaneous writing has not been re-worked, it can prove very powerful because what has been written at the time of upset, anxiety or distress will describe raw feelings and emotions. Because this was a piece of freewriting, I didn't feel a need to do anything else with it. The purpose was served in a way that is similar to my journal writing in that I do not have to worry about any technical aspect of the writing. This is very liberating. There is nothing to stop me taking what has been written and polishing it into a finished piece of work, but then not striving for a perfect finished piece of writing is healing in itself.

I have noticed that since writing about my patient, I am also a part of the process. My writing not only connects me to the person I write about but also opens a door into my own inner world. This has given me a space to explore my connection to my writing.

Although I wrote the above piece for someone else, I am not totally disconnected from the outcome because, as with any of my writing, there is always a part of me held within the lines.

Creating a Legacy Out of Everyday Living *Claire Willis*

For the last ten years, I have facilitated writing groups for people who were living with and dying from cancer. I choose this work because of the immediacy with which people live when they know they don't have 'forever'. Like my group members, I often wondered how I would be remembered and what kind of difference my life was making, often writing about these questions in my journal, and simultaneously wondering about the purpose of these entries.

Then I attended a workshop in Minneapolis offered by Rachael Freed based on her book *Women's Lives, Women's Legacies* (2003). There I was introduced to a new way of holding these questions and making meaning. Since then, I have been teaching and personally using these techniques for creating a legacy in my own work and with people living with cancer.

Freed identified six universal needs that legacy writing addresses: the need to belong, to be known, to be remembered, to have our lives make a difference, to be blessed and to bless and celebrate life.

We began by making a list of instructions or messages, implicit or explicit, that we had received from our family, community or religious training. We were then asked to make another list of instructions that we might want to leave for future generations – our children, a partner, close friends or relatives.

My list included the following:

Be generous and give anonymously.

Stay thin and watch what you eat.

Find work in which your passion and the world's needs intersect.

Always take into consideration others' feelings.

We were asked to convert these instructions or messages into blessings using stems that might include some of the following: *May you always… May God or your higher power… May you be blessed as I have been with… I wish for you… I hope for you…*

We reframed our instructions into blessings using a stem from above. We selected for our focus one of our blessings, making certain that we had not just rewritten an instruction. For example, my instruction: *Be generous and give anonymously* was initially converted to a blessing as: *May you find a way to give anonymously.*

Rereading this, I realised that it still sounded like an instruction, and that I had not really 'softened' the language sufficiently. I had written it from my mind instead of my heart. I rewrote it: *May you always be guided through life by generosity and the capacity to give without having to be known or seen for your gifts.*

In my rewrite, I could feel how the language I chose softened, not only the message but something inside me as well. The harshness of the instruction became a wish for my children to do something differently from me. I wanted to save them from a sorrow I had experienced. I could even feel grief in my body as I wrote it and knew that there was a great deal of feeling behind that initial instruction. I could not just tell my children to do something differently, rather I needed to share how I learned that lesson.

I asked myself why I had chosen this particular blessing. I wondered what was behind my particular wish to pass this along. Then I wrote the story from my life from which this instruction and blessing had come, trying to write from my heart and not my head.

The writing stirred a great deal of grief in myself.

> May you always be guided through life by generosity and the capacity to give without having to be known. Several years ago, I facilitated week-long residential retreats for people living with cancer. At the end of the week, I donated my salary back to the sponsoring non-profit. I enjoyed the gratitude that came my way. I loved this little grass roots group. In addition

to donating my salary back, I made a monthly donation on my credit card for a number of years following my work there. After a while, I decided I would stop the monthly giving and find a local non-profit that did similar work I called the director, a friend of mine, and explained my decision.

Weeks later, I received a phone call from the director, inviting me to return to the retreat centre to again facilitate a week-long retreat. I wondered if they wanted me to come again because they hoped that I would donate more money or whether it was because they wanted my facilitation skills. That persistent question led me to decide, like your grandfather had always done, to only donate money anonymously. My relationships now are more protected from my own questions, insecurities and fears. While I may miss the acknowledgement that can come from making donations, the clarity of my relationships feels much more important and I have found a way to protect myself from myself and those lingering questions.

Completing this exercise, I realised that I had learned a way to share life experiences and convert them into a legacy for my loved ones. It gave me a way to work with sorrows, to explore my mistakes and my strengths. It gave me a container for reflection and it helped me transform wishes for others into blessings for others, inviting me to look inside to explore why a specific instruction or blessing was so important to me. Where did my heart need to soften and break open a little more? Where had it been broken and need healing or new meaning? Where might there be a possible teaching for myself or others?

Legacies are vehicles to pass on hard earned heart filled wisdom and experiences to those we love and will leave behind. What better way to show our love?

———•◆•———

CHAPTER 5

Writing the Troubled Self

Edited by Victoria Field

At times of crisis, depression and difficulty, many people find that personal writing can be a way of imposing structure on chaos. It can create a safe 'container' into which feelings, that might otherwise become overwhelming, can be poured.

Rebecca Atherton finds that she needs to freewrite and journal during periods of depression and also at other times to maintain health and well-being. As well as offering catharsis, the process provides her with material to shape into poems. Rose Flint describes the long process of sculpting a specific poem written at a time of loss and unhappiness. Her account documents the initial burst of writing that was followed by a process of crafting and paying attention to what the poem wants to say. The final stand-alone poem can still surprise her with new insights years later.

As well as being a tool to help with current difficulties, personal writing can illuminate the past. Yona McGinnis finds that comparing two pieces of writing from different periods of her life can 'give perspective', encouragement and comfort in difficult times. Maggie Sawkins adopts a Japanese form to write about 'No Man's Land', in both its political sense and her own experience of living there metaphorically 'for years'. As is so often the case, the constraints of writing in form can paradoxically liberate the writer.

The final piece is by three theatre practitioners who each wrote a fairy tale as a way of finding empathy and diversity of insight with women who self-harm. Entering into an imaginative space where they could experience feelings directly, rather than theorising, gave them material on which to base an educational piece of theatre.

Cracks *Rebecca Atherton*

Not so long ago, I was in a pretty bad place emotionally, suffering from depression and debilitating panic attacks. Relying on pills to function, I was only half present and sleeping excessively. Fearing my ability to cope in the world, and having come to view my company as feeble at best, I seldom left the house and refused to see anyone. It took all of my reserves of energy just to stand upright, and even then I only shuffled octogenarian-like from bed to bathroom and back. I couldn't read. I couldn't write. I couldn't even listen to the radio. Naturally creative, I felt like I had been imprisoned inside my own head.

I can't remember exactly when, but I woke up one morning and realised that I was stuck in this negative cycle and had been for a while. Determined to break out of it before it became 'the story of the rest of my life', I began to see a therapist. Understanding the background behind my condition and having someone to talk to helped, but I was still a long way from where I needed to be and growing impatient.

Having researched the creative therapies in the past and applied the techniques of both journal and poetry therapy to my writing, I decided to set myself a fresh project: something small and accessible that I could carry with me at all times; something to accompany me on this journey and bear testament to it afterwards. I started to write a thought diary and filled it with personal essays, poetry and prose, using it to explore my mind instinctively rather than rationally.

Although initially crippled by the partners of depression – depleted self-confidence and lack of drive – with perseverance, I confronted each new obstacle and fought my way through. Trusting myself and writing without editing was the key to this process. It was only through really listening to myself and documenting what I had to say, without judgement, that I heard what needed to be said and was able to honour it. Gradually, by switching my medication to regular doses of reading and writing, and by making a conscious effort to be a better mother to myself, I exited the dark box I had been inhabiting and climbed the long ladder back to life. In the end, this vehicle for a metaphorical step back became all I needed to locate those first tentative steps on the road to self-knowledge, self-acceptance and self-love. My writing showed me I wasn't alone in my suffering, my situation wasn't unique and that others had gone before me and survived. 'Cracks' was one of the first pieces to emerge during this period of awakening and writing it was a pivotal moment for me.

Cracks
Something must have visited me as I slept,
Slamming balled fists
Into the gentle rise and fall of my chest,
For awake I cannot move
And everything hurts.

A warm bottle hugs me tight
Filling in for the embrace of pills.
Rocking it, I conjure up a child,
Rewinding the circle of grief,
Turning the emptiness inside out.

Reluctant to break the spell,
I look to the wall and count cracks
Searching for answers to questions about myself.
You watch me in black and white –
Sad, because there is nothing you can do.

The process I used to unlock this poem, and the other pieces of writing that followed, is called freewriting and I like it because it is a gentle way of tapping into and releasing blocked issues and emotions. It is also quick, easily practised, and an excellent portal for discovering themes and subjects that can then be used as material for further writing.

When doing this writing, the first thing I do is find a place to sit. Depending on my mood, it can be anywhere from the kitchen table to under a tree at the bottom of the garden. I then ask myself how long I am able to spend on this task, remaining flexible as to the answer. Experience has taught me not to apply pressure or it becomes overly daunting. Equally, without an element of challenge, nothing of any value is achieved. On bad days, I might only manage three minutes. Better days, I can extend this to ten.

Next I begin to write. The only rules are that I don't pause, think, reread or edit until my time is up – to do so interferes with the flow of words. On finishing, I sit back and take a few moments to honour my achievement. When ready, I read back over what I have written, looking for messages within the text. Something generally stands out as particularly poignant. I use this in the next stage. On a fresh sheet of paper, writing loosely without influencing the words too much, trusting my subconscious to do the real work, I start to analyse it. Finally, I select a form, usually poetry, and begin to tighten this up. Often it helps to distance myself, transforming my thoughts and feelings into abstract or inanimate imagery.

Reading over what I have written teaches me a lot, providing the insight necessary to make vital changes or begin the process of deeper work. This holds true whenever I return to the piece, be it days or months later: there is always more to be learnt, even if now in hindsight.

Writing in this way has transformed my life. In times of adversity I have a tendency to shut down, a defence mechanism that backfires until it has become the opposite of recovery. I have learnt that in order for me to remain both emotionally and physically healthy, I have to make a conscious effort to document how I feel. Whether it is just a few words in a journal, the first line of a poem, or a complete story, every word that makes it out onto the page is a step in the right direction.

For me, writing serves multiple purposes. In the moment of crisis it provides comfort and catharsis. Later, rereading reveals a greater perspective, leading to understanding, acceptance and recovery. One piece becomes another and another until the problem is resolved, or at least exorcised to the extent that I can return to my life. Ultimately, I find it comforting to know that I possess the strength inside to overcome the darkness that descends. Remembering this in times of trial saves me from returning to that dark cell.

The Blue Gate *Rose Flint*

It was a year of uncertain weather. I had moved to Bath and felt unhappy living in a city, missing the Welsh Borders. I was also beginning my menopause, experiencing deep wild moods, no elation. From this depressed place I began working on my third book *Nekyia* (Flint 2003), trying to make some sense of my emotional roller-coaster, my deep sense of loss. I had written a number of poems which I realised were the beginning of a sequence; some kind of inner journey that I was making, trying to reach 'home'. Some were autobiographical, some were complete fictions, or bits of both together.

In the Odyssey, 'Nekyia' is the word used to describe a 'Night Sea Journey' – a time of descending through darkness and danger, into the underworld. There are many other myths of the journey – Persephone lost in Hades or Inanna going down through seven gates to find her dark sister Erishkagil. For many people who suffer from depression, the word 'descent' is a very real descriptive term and, for some women, the onset of age and the changes it brings are also experienced negatively as a kind of lessening of self, an alteration of direction that leads only to death.

One morning, I woke to find the world white with snow and realised that I would not be going to drive to Wales as planned. Snow has a magical light. It makes things possible. I found myself alone in the house, drifting around, enjoying a sudden sense of weightlessness, no pressure, time out. After a while though, I knew I wanted to write, that it was important to do it right away. I sat by the window in my room, looking out at the great fat snowflakes still drifting down onto the white-laden trees, the still world of back gardens and sheds ...*and the poem came in from somewhere else, over my left shoulder and across my body down my right arm, into my hand...*

I wrote solidly for maybe 20 minutes although it felt longer. I was not at all conscious of the words as they came and I did not pause. I was aware that I was deliberately allowing this – as in the exercise of 'Secret Writing' when you put your pen at the top of the page and write for a pre-determined time. I use this technique a lot and value it highly for making conscious what is deeply held in unknowing.

The poem that 'arrived' was 'The Blue Gate' (Flint 2003, p.69) or at least half of it. It was eventually the most central poem in the collection and is certainly the most important to me. In that first piece of writing

I felt very fused to some inner centre which gave me vision. The first-person narrative of the piece is structured in several parts. I am in a snow-filled park, beside a swan, feeling fearful about ageing. The poem then moves into the vision of a Being walking across ice towards me – a Swan-Woman, old and wrinkled.

> Palms upward, she stretches her hands out towards me,
> black bird-eyes intent.
> She is holding pieces of ice and she strikes them together
> slowly at first, then gathering speed
> so they clash edgily, ring like bronze bells
> over the ice-field: a call, a warning of breakage,
> rupture, opening.
> In the cold heart of her handfuls of ice
> sparks flick scarlet snake-tongues that rise and grow,
> so ice warms, whitefire on her palms, candles of crystal.
> She draws the radiance into her body, lets it wander
> the routes of her veins, the web of her cells
> until she stands gilded, feathers on fire, sun in her skin.
> Walking past me her feet melt bird-tracks on the snow.
> She is going deeper, and at the point where distance
> takes her, there is a spreading cloud of blue.

And that was as far as I could go. Whatever was happening stopped and I could not continue to write. I knew there was a second part of the poem but I could not reach it – not by thinking, nor by trying to get to it through more unconscious processes.

And that was how things stayed for months. But I kept going back to it, the image was so powerful for me that I could see the gaze in the Swan-Woman's eyes. *Look at me*, she said, *Look at me*.

So I did. I meditated on the image, slowly learning what she brought. I began to come to terms with my own changes, to own them fully and in that take on a deeper understanding of Death. I stopped being so afraid of ageing, stopped believing that love would die, that my inner fires of joy and creativity would go out. There had been something stalled in me. Depression and loss had brought me to a point of being *petrified*: I was stone, immovable in fear in a grey world.

Reading the poem today, I was surprised to notice two lines in the first part: *Who will come to me with apples in her hand, / honey loaves, a bowl of light? Who will warm me?* I remember that crying voice, wanting comfort. Then the answer, the vision of Swan-Woman, not comfortable, but powerful certainly, releasing fire from ice.

This first part of the poem remained virtually unedited. It took about nine months to write the second half, with dozens of drafts. It was hard, like sculpting granite; every draft was hewing out meaning. My writing altered as I began to take the 'journey' forward, instead of looking backwards and grieving all the time. I think that the vision, the meditation and then the work were all necessary processes that I needed to go through to shift the depression.

Giving Perspective *Yona McGinnis*

Feelings of alone can isolate me.
Feelings of bad or crazy can too.

I find myself perched on the edge of alone over and over again. The borders are hazy here. There is no light, no day or night. Everything is coloured by the hues of my uncertainty. These thousands of moments in my life, of feeling 'stuck-in-alone', when I was sure that no one has ever felt as 'apart-from' as me, have resulted in hundreds of poems that poured themselves from my gut.

The poems externalised my feelings, making space to be filled as more horror filled my inner being. The fear and anger gathered with the force of a gale, ready to unleash all its power and fury. When there were no poems, the storm railed inward. The poems were the keepers of my secrets, and my release. They lay dormant, under the bed accumulating with the rest of the rubbish of my past. As I dared to unearth the poems, dusty with living under the bed for so long, I also began to use my voice. At first it was a whisper, barely audible above the sound of my own pounding pulse, and then a throaty growl pierced the silence I used to shield myself from the consequences of 'telling'. Finally, came the howls and triumphant, chest-thumping roars – as loud and strong as any I've ever heard in a Tarzan movie. That voice gave me the courage to share my poetry, which for me, was a bridge to healing and connection.

I wrote reflectively about my poetry:

> An image that appears throughout my writing, is that of feeling alone, apart, separate from the rest of the world. I needed the sense of being heard, of sharing my reality, before the images I had painted so clearly for decades, could lead – or drag – me to full awareness and realisation of who I was and what the pictures meant. So as I nudged myself back and forth, and from side to side, I explored the ideas that would eventually offer me my own salvation through ever-growing volumes of poetry.
>
> (July 2008)

In 'stuck' times of poring over old poems and thumbing through old journals, I'd say aloud to myself, 'I may not be in a great place now, but at least I'm not back there.' I read the evidence of healing that runs through my writing. Even in my blackest moments, I have peered through the lines of my poetry, and the spaces in between, and felt healing energy as they connected me to the moment.

Laid out end to end, my poems are a life map that shows me where I have been and where I might go. The regressions and sideways movement are there too, evidence of times of overwhelming distress. I began to see them as affirmations of the inner work I have done.

I developed a technique I call 'giving perspective'. It is an exercise designed to help me look at where I was and where I am now. It reminds me that movement is not only possible, but is really happening, enabling me to feel un-stuck and connected in relationship. This involves a process of re-framing. In reflecting on two or more pieces of past work, I naturally recall past feelings and can also glimpse the connections that pull me forward.

By working with any two pieces of writing, whether from journals, presentations or anything I have written passionately from the heart, I can give myself an opportunity to gain perspective on the place I am in now, whether it is 'stuck-ness' or some other version of drying up that may have sucked the creativity from my hand, voice or lips. For me, such writing was done sometimes on the backs of napkins at a coffee shop, or while waiting for my children, when the words that gave form to my pain came spontaneously. The two pieces need not have been written decades apart but should be from times that 'feel' different, or, conversely, feel too much the same.

The suggestion I follow is to write reflectively about my feelings, sensations and thoughts as I re-read my work and to allow myself to reflect positively on where I am now. I write until I feel done – this may come in the form of poetry or prose.

For example, the following extracts from two poems written seven years apart show a great change in perspective.

> … My mind reels
> With the explosion of confused sensations.
> I am unable to contain the thoughts,
> They belong to the world
> Not to me.

> **SELF**
> I am a mother.
> My sons love living,
> They need to know that all is right in the world.
> My daughter is the woman
> I would have wanted to be
> Thirty years ago.
> I teach yoga. I stand on my head
> And see the world
> The way it was meant to be…

> I am a mother.
> I give birth
> Over and over
> Again.

A year later I reflected that: '…having healed from childhood scars, recovered from eating disorders and flourished as a mother and teacher, [I find] being able to see all that in a record of poetry is unusually inspiring…'

The Year the Wall Came Down *Maggie Sawkins*

The year the wall came down I found myself in No Man's Land. Looking through a photograph album with a friend, I came across an old picture of myself standing in front of the Berlin Wall. My friend remarked on the stanchion that could be seen poking through the rubble and suggested that the photograph would be a good subject for a poem. I hadn't written anything for a while and my imagination was hungry for a trigger. Once my friend had left, I sat quietly with the photograph in my hand.

Through a hole in the wall I could see No Man's Land. I remembered it as a place I had known well – I had been living there for years. In 1989, the year the wall came down, I was a mature student studying for a degree in English with Art, and loved it. It provided a haven from my home life where everything was going wrong. My marriage was failing, my elder daughter was troubled, and the effects of my mother's emotional dependency on me seemed something I'd never escape from. I felt like boarding a train and never getting off. When the opportunity of a ten-day field trip to Berlin to study Expressionism arose, I jumped.

My usual mode of expression is poetry. Recently, however, I've become interested in the haibun, a Japanese word meaning 'poetry prose'. I find the form offers a way of structuring some of my notebooks' abandoned scribble and meanderings. The original Japanese haibun style was created by the Japanese poet-monk Basho and tended to focus on his wanderings through Japan. Some have described haibun as a narrative of an epiphany, but many haibun are simply narratives of special moments in a person's life. The one or more haiku that accompany haibun prose are of two types. The first summarises the feel of the prose, but without repeating words or phrases or images already contained in the prose. The haiku may be a juxtaposition – seemingly different yet connected. The second is a haiku that moves beyond the prose passage taking the reader yet one step further in the narrative.

After writing down the title 'The Year the Wall Came Down', the opening sentence followed like a gift. 'No Man's Land', the phrase, the place, the state of mind offered both a metaphorical and an emotional connection. Seduced by its poetic resonance, I was eager to include the word 'stanchion' and so I began with a simple description of the photographic scene. Tapping into the most potent memories of the time helped to drive the narrative forward. The emerging theme of political and personal displacement is reflected in the choice of imagery: the 'upstroke of a stranger's name', the scene inside the museum, the incident at the telephone kiosk. The appearance of the young woman in the bar, who represented the old me, brought the piece to a close. I had arrived at a place of emotional truth. The process of finding the right words to recount a forgotten experience had enabled me to get in touch with a part of my psyche that I thought had been left behind. It also made me realise how far I had moved on in my emotional life.

Coming back to my writing a few days later, I pondered on how I could successfully incorporate a haiku, to find an image that was 'different' but 'connected'. It was an enjoyable challenge and eventually I found one that seemed to link the political with the personal, to 'take the reader yet one step further'. Once I was satisfied that the piece was complete, I began to read it aloud to check for ease of expression, clichés, crispness of vocabulary, syntax. I made a few changes, and a couple more after taking the piece to a poetry workshop.

'The Year the Wall Came Down' could so easily not have been written. It could have remained as a snapshot of memory, or notes categorised as a piece of rambling, unworthy material for a poem. The haibun offered a structure, on the borderline between prose and poetry, into which a forgotten voice could venture and be heard.

> I found myself in No Man's Land. Sir took a photograph of me posing in front of twisted stanchion and rubble. A few yards away people were sitting behind trestle tables selling fragments of the wall. I picked a piece marked with faded red paint from the ground. I wondered if once it had been the upstroke of a stranger's name.

> In the afternoon Sir took us to the museum. I stayed the whole time in Casper David Friedrich's room looking at a painting of a monk standing on the edge of a vast still sea. It was so unlike home where waves crashed against walls.

> After supper I stood for a moment in the queue by the telephone kiosk, then wandered into the hostel bar. Apart from the barman, the room was empty. I caught a glimpse of a young woman in the mirror opposite, her eyes another country. She was staring straight through me to a place without corners – a place where no one knew your scent, your name.

> Carried by the tide
> to an anonymous shore –
> a coil of barbed wire.

> (Sawkins 2008, p.6)

Stories from the Silk Tent *Lucy O'Hagan, Gilly Pugh, Lizzi Yates*

The Silk Tent Company is a theatre company located in Wanaka, a small town in New Zealand's Southern Alps. In 2008 we received a New Zealand Mental Health Foundation Media Grant to devise a piece of theatre on self-mutilation. The result was 'Girl With No Words – listening to the language of cutting', a multimedia performance involving drama, documentary, fairy tale, poetry, song and drawings.

Our aim was to get our audience to think. About the experience of self-harm and about people's reaction to it. We are interested in compassion and what it is to stand alongside someone in their suffering.

We chose self-mutilation, (also known as self-injury, self-harm or cutting), because it is a complex and uncomfortable issue. It happens in all communities. It carries shame and stigma for those who hurt themselves.

We talked to many people who have or are self-injuring. We read widely and researched the literature. We talked about our own experience of and response to self-injury. We saw that self-injury is essentially voiceless. The person who cuts usually can't speak their despair. Our problem was how to represent a voiceless experience on stage.

We tried some creative writing exercises to find the words and form we could use for script-writing. We started with a six-minute freewriting exercise, writing anything that came into our heads about any topic as fast as possible without lifting the pen. We were amazed how much this uncluttered our minds, so that most of the subsequent writing seemed to flow easily onto the page.

We then spent ten minutes each creating a list of single words that related to self-injury, working quickly without editing or correcting. The word lists seemed to unlock a vocabulary for the self-injured.

Lizzi

53 words starting with blood and ending with touch. I think in pictures and I saw the single words tracking a line like an incision down the centre of the page before I began to write. It seemed to me that the words were as isolated as someone self-harming, compressed into a format they couldn't escape.

As a young child she had been sent to live with an elderly couple who were famous for training princesses. Unfortunately, the old man had taken to gambling. His creditors suggested that they did not want their money so long as they could touch the princess. Every day the men would come and touch the princess in a locked room in the castle. The princess was terrified as she knew that the touching was bad and with every touch she felt the badness oozing into her.

She knew that no one would hear her screams as even though the old woman was kind, she was deaf. She tried to tell the men to stop but she was so terrified she could not speak. She tried to appeal to the old man with her eyes but he would not look at her.

She managed as best she could. She would leave her body for the men to touch and take her soul into the ceiling of the room out of their reach. And when they left, she looked at her body and it seemed to be dirty and bloody but she picked it up and cleaned it and put it back on…but it became harder and harder to put it on for her soul was growing through its suffering and her body was still that of a small child.

And her body lost all feeling. Sometimes she would clasp her beautiful hand around a rose bush to see if she could feel the thorns pierce her skin. And although she did not feel the thorns, when she saw the blood she realised she was real and her body did belong to her soul and she felt at great peace. And in the end the only way she could be at peace was to pierce her skin and see her own blood…

But as the years passed she began to show kindness to herself in the way she showed kindness to others. She learned over time to love and care for her body and gradually her body seemed to fit more easily with her soul and she did not need to see her blood to know that her body was hers.

Lucy reflects: I wrote this piece without stopping or correcting and really had no idea where it was going to go. I knew that the fairy tale allowed for exploration of difficult subjects anchored by happy endings. There was both freedom and safety in this.

We talked about fairy tales having the illusion of distance. They are written in the third person, and they are not set in real time or a real place. They are not 'true' stories. This was helpful to me as I had anxiety about trying to portray someone else's experience, that in trying to speak for others I might get it wrong. But with the illusion of distance, one can get very close to a truth. I was conscious of wanting to honour all of the princess's story so people could feel the horror of it and understand her need to self-harm. It felt like such a big, burdensome and complex story and afterwards I was physically drained and traumatised. I think that in writing the princess's story I had discovered a great deal of empathy with it. I am a doctor and for me empathy requires a creative imagining of someone else's experience. Somehow the metaphor inherent in fairy tales seems to unlock the necessary imaginative sensory space.

This piece was read by the protagonist at the end of the performance as she reveals her own childhood sexual abuse through drawing and fairy tale.

Lizzi reflects: As the self-designated non-writer in our group I was dubious as to how useful anything I might write could be to our theatre project. Intrigued by the idea of using a fairy tale to tell a tale of self-injury, I was also frightened. I knew how difficult it was to unlock possibility whilst marooned in a self-injurious mind-body state. I couldn't see how I might ever regard self-harm other than with shame. With hindsight, I see how the struggle to articulate a silenced story brings the teller of the story into a new relationship with the experience.

My interest was in metamorphosis, the magical power of transformation that spins straw into gold, brings about impossible change. How would the story find the happy ending, the promise of future?

Lizzi's tale was about a small and happy prince who is overwhelmed by catastrophe. The adults in the prince's life are benign. When the prince tells his father about the catastrophe, all the king's horses and all the kings men were summoned to help. There is a sense of many people involved with and caring for the prince and his happiness. This is *not* common in stories of self-injury.

> *Lizzi reflects:* I later knew this was not enough, the story could not finish with external help. Part of me hoped the story would disappear and I could excuse myself with declaring that words were not my medium. But the story would not leave me alone. After several days I went back to the text and rapidly wrote the ending.

Lizzi's fairy tale (extract)

The players were deeply moved and wanted to help the boy and to free the monster from his curse. They made a great fire and cooked a great feast, and then they performed their best stories for the boy and creature, singing and jesting and telling tales of wonder. And the prince found life returning to his limbs and the wounds that he had inflicted on himself began to fade.

He turned to face the monster beside him who seemed less frightening and, after all this time, strangely familiar. Taking pity, he reached for the creature and touched its rheumy eyes gently with his finger, releasing a quantity of tears. The boy recognised the suffering as his own, and kissed the face behind the tears.

The idea of transformation was important in our theatre piece. We wanted to convey a sense of hope and the possibility of well-being. Responses from others to self-injury are often hostile and can perpetuate a cycle of desperation. The travelling troupe played out an alternative story for the prince conveyed with kindness, respect, hope and humour. In writing the play we saw that the protagonist had to locate some kindness, hope and compassion for herself. Just as the prince recognised the monster as his own suffering.

We read our stories to each other. The words 'once upon a time' opened us up to receive the stories with a child-like innocence. The story seemed to have a life of its own sitting in the liminal space between the teller and the listener, as if we were reading something written by someone else.

Writing fairy tales moved us as a group from a theoretical to a creative space, by moving us inside the experience of self-mutilation. And we realised we had begun script-writing.

CHAPTER 6

Our Families, Ourselves

Edited by Gillie Bolton

A rich variety of ways of rediscovering, reliving and healing family memories are explained and explicated below. Linda Sliwoski's method was to focus directly on a significant event in order to pin it in her memory in as full detail as possible. Glynis Charlton used writing to enable her to overcome a block in her emotional development by using freewriting to allow anger to spill onto the page, creating a draft she could work on. She made lists, explored the metaphors which arose, made use of the published poetry of others, and listened for meaningful phrases in unlikely places which became writing openers. Marliss Weber created lists of memory elements, mining recollections for beneficial healing associations. Margot Van Sluytman tells us how reading poetry enabled her to trust her pen to the page, and her writing eventually led to reconciliation with her father's murderer, and involvement in writing and restorative justice.

Nigel Gibbons and Jonathan Knight used effective extended metaphors to enable them to get close to feelings: turning the abstraction of bereavement into a concrete object or event which seemed to personify their fathers. Like Graham Hartill, who also gained from researching the circumstances of his forbears, they explain the power of redrafting for clarification and gaining contact with depth of feeling. Jonathan exhorts writers to save their drafts to be worked on later. Nigel significantly explains how the act of writing a life story changes us.

Time Capsule *Linda Sliwoski*

> The Time Capsule is a versatile tool that reviews the activities of your life and structures them into a cohesive story. A Time Capsule in journal writing captures the essence of your life as it was being lived at a given moment. Time Capsule entries are periodic logs written on a daily, weekly, monthly, even quarterly basis.
>
> (Adams 1990, p.159)

I chose to use the Time Capsule method on this occasion because I wanted to capture a particular time. This journal technique is useful, I find, because it depicts a story or memory I do not want to forget.

This moment was pivotal in the lives of both my daughter and me. The natural separation from child to young adult was captured, like a photograph. I closed my eyes and envisioned this particular event, so that it felt vivid, as if I was present. I used my five senses: hearing, smell, sight, taste, touch.

I use a Time Capsule whenever I experience a transformational or an 'aha' moment such as: the birth of a child, the death of a parent, a graduation, my wedding day. Sometimes this transformational moment is not a significant life event. It is always an experience which had a major impact on my thinking, feeling or functioning.

> *August 2008: Alannah, Romania, where to begin?*
> I wanted to be brave like you. My back pack was too heavy. Yours was light. You carried only what you needed, I too much. Our mission: plant a seed, give hope and show love; as American missionaries to Romanian orphans.
>
> The ride to the mountains; unexplainable! The country-side felt warm with repeating fields of sunflowers calling out to welcome us. We saw a gypsy man and little girl on a wagon packed with their possessions being pulled by an old mule.

The final dirt road to our camp was dry and dusty. The houses were crowded together but neatly cared for. Their front doors caught my eye, each different. Each had a story. There, ours was unfolding. Orphans greeted us with open arms. Excitement filled the air. With three children wrapped around your body, your fragile heart was displayed as you wiggled your hand free and in sign language said: 'I love you.' Sign language became our way of connecting in this foreign country. Moments I will never forget; the human touch and the presence of caring for God's children connected us.

The children bonded with you instantly. Your gifts of acceptance and being present in each situation during the week impressed me. Your laughter was infectious. I was humbled by your unconditional love.

The orphans needed so much physical contact. You and I had very little physical contact and I was more comfortable with this than ever imagined. We were separating as mother and child. I was experiencing my 'little girl' growing up. What a gift this was, I was in the moment!

Reflection: I met who you have become in Romania. You live in the moment, are independent and open to life's experiences. I appreciate you for who you are; a strong-willed, goal-oriented, but simple woman. You taught me to live by faith and to leave 'life's baggage' in Romania.

When Melancholia Strikes, Poetry Steps In *Glynis Charlton*

When my father lay dying, I felt the hospital air was heavy with meaningful phrases, like thick poetry soup, although I'm predominantly a prose writer. My mother, racked with bitterness at half a century of lost opportunities, angered me immeasurably with her self-pity. I'd booked onto the UK National Association of Writers in Education retreat at The Hurst in Shropshire to work on my novel and was worried that this anger, coupled with my inability to ladle up Dad's poetry soup, would block me from a productive week. I knew I needed a good old rant, so gave myself permission to do just that and spent a couple of nights at a remote farmhouse in deepest Shropshire, leading up to the retreat.

Poetry so often begins for me with a phrase leaping out. This time it was the farm owner, who was 'overtired'. What a strange expression. I knew just what she meant, but how would we define it? When I began to explore the feeling, I remembered being overtired as a child, described as being 'past myself', and how there was nothing to be done, but to give in to it – only by shutting out the world could I feel right again. This was the kick-start I'd needed. Let the rant begin.

My anger spilled out onto ten sides of A5. I realised the ranting had thrown up some useful analogies and lessons learned, which I extracted as statements addressed to Mum:

> I am your overtired child longing to sleep
> I want to shut you out like the lids of that pot doll with the nylon lashes
> I want to bag you up like the bin liners I stuffed with years of your cushions, your antimacassars, a shammy [chamois] leather unopened, 7/6d
> I hate that frown, that gathering of eight decades of lines, queuing up to throw arrows at me like a legion of Roman soldiers, rank upon rank
> I will allow my own legion to stride down the hillside to meet yours, no longer holding back, but threatening, exhaling the truth
> I hate your generated paraphernalia – three pairs of tweezers, 15 purses containing £66 worth of small change
> I was a plant, picked by a man and kept in the same kind of pot as you – cracked and cheap and considered worthless
> I am as wild as a dog rose and you bleat like a sheep [the Shropshire landscape creeping in]
> You taught me how to bake a cake, how to give up my seat on the bus, but never how a person actually has Choices.
> You can squirrel away money, hide bank statements behind cushions and fivers in secret compartments, but you can't stash opportunities and time
> You're trying to make me feel bad for living my life. Well, I refuse to.

This process led me to think of all that can be left unsaid when a person dies. I'd had the privilege of saying goodbye properly to both my sister and my dad but was worried that my anger would prevent me from one day doing the same with my mum.

I decided to re-read some of Sharon Olds' collected poems. Her poignant description of watching herself in the mirror as she brushes her daughter's hair (2005, p.23) has always moved me. I pondered over the issue of mothers leaving their lives behind while their daughters continued with their own.

Before long, my mother would probably leave. I placed myself in a mirror and returned to early adolescence, eventually recalling how she loved to relax in her armchair after Sunday lunch as I stood behind her, smoothing Ponds Cold Cream onto her skin. Those Roman legion frowns became my starting point. I thought about childhood innocence and began listing different perceptions, under the heading: 'When you are little you do not see...'

an army of soldiers	you see	a frown
a person being bagged/planted etc	you see	just the person
throwing away time	you see	boredom
guilt	you see	punishment/atonement

I played around with these for a while but nothing was emerging (although the one around guilt interested me), finally drafting a short poem that began with 'pacifying the Roman legions'. Again, this wasn't working, but it did point me to the right track and I eventually found that, totally unbidden, coming through the anger was a certain sadness, almost a reconciliation through poetry:

> Your life in bin bags,
> heading for the charity shop
> a chamois leather seven shillings new
> and fifteen purses clasping sixteen pounds
> forty-three; and it's there –
> at the back of the drawer,
> behind the earrings you hadn't worn
> for years – Ponds Cold Cream. Yellowed,
> hardened. I dab my fingers in the jar

and feel once more the pull of your skin
as I smooth it over your face;
our Sunday scene, before carverys came,
with all the shops shut and
some old film on the telly.

It's like a Pearl & Dean ad;
happy mother, daughter, brought together
by the Whole Nut treat and Gregory Peck...
My father's advice arrives from the greenhouse:
'you can't take it with you –
when you're gone, that's your lot.'

I had given myself permission to rant, but I found I'd also given myself permission to live my life as I wished. And there, totally unexpected, was my father – just a sip of the poetry soup enough to let me move on. I went to The Hurst and immersed myself in working on my novel.

The Legacy of Mothers *Marliss Weber*

As a newly married woman, my mind has turned to families: the family of my birth, the family I have joined through my husband, and the family my husband and I will create. I wonder about what kind of parent I will be, what legacy I will pass on, what legacy I have inherited from my mother and her mother.

In order to explore this idea of legacy on paper, I used a 'webbing' process, jotting down and connecting the clearest memories I have of my grandmother – the delicious bread she baked, her obsession with dolls, her wonderful storytelling ability and the warm attention she paid to me as a little girl. These memories helped me place my grandmother in a positive context and forced me to look at her as an individual in her own right, a woman of much more than the label 'grandmother' allows. Before this process, I hadn't thought of her as a woman like me, she was always just 'grandma'. This process helped me to see beyond this label and love the woman of skill and talent that she was.

Next, I focused on the memories I have of my mother, trying to crystallise her essence in a few words, describing her own special skills. My mother, the great organiser, the educator, the creator, and also the free spirit, full of fun – these are the words that came to me to describe her. And images sprang to mind as well: her perfectly ordered cupboards and her immaculate house – the same immaculate house her mother kept as well.

And then, I considered my skills, my talents, and a wonderful pattern emerged. Without recognising it, knowing it, I found that I am a terrific blend of the women who came before me. My mother has passed along her passion for literature, her mother her love of stories (or 'lies', as she called them). We all sew and decorate and can make something out of nothing, and cook and clean and express ourselves with words.

My mother and her own mother were not close. My mother craved a confidante in her mother, a cheerleader, a champion. And although my grandmother was a kind and loving woman, she grew distant with age, dwelling on past disappointments and slights, rather than giving my mother the positive attention that, even in her forties and fifties, she needed from her parent.

My mother and I are close. She is my best friend, my cheerleader and champion. But we're very different people, as different as she was from her own mother. Looking at us all as individuals – these three generations of women – it's hard to see the family connections. The differences in values and beliefs create a gulf between the generations, which this writing sought to bridge:

Legacy

Things my Grandmother could do:
Bake the most delicious sweet dough bread that
You'd never believe came from a recipe
And not her head.
Weave wigs for dolls out of her own hair
And others, mine as well,
And crochet an afghan in under a week.
Tell stories and lies at young girls' tea parties
And sew dresses for daughters and dolls from
The same fabric.
Build furniture for children and clean everything,
Including under the rim of the sink
Sometimes with a toothpick.

Things my Mother can do:
Sew curtains and pillows and arrange flowers
And paint the living room
All in an afternoon.
Correct essays and grammar and read novels
Of Britain while
Sitting on the floor watching American Idol.
Organize closets and cupboards with
White plastic trays of colour-coded pens and
Notepads and paintbrushes and papers.
And clean everything,
Including under the rim of the sink
Sometimes with a toothpick.

Things I can do:
Tell stories and lies for young girls at tea parties.
Sew curtains and pillows and correct essays and grammar
And crochet an afghan in a bit more than a week.
Bake the most delicious bread from a recipe you'd never
Believe came from a book,
From a shelf organized by author and alphabet.
Watch American Idol while composing a poem
And arrange flowers and furniture and paint the living room
And clean everything,
Including under the rim of the sink
Sometimes with a toothpick.

This poem expresses the connections I now feel to these two significant women in my life. I feel grounded in my family experience and I'm proud of these connections. In this process, I have also found a sense of redemption: a feeling of understanding and love for my grandmother that I hadn't felt since I was a child.

I feel privileged to have come from such a strong, resourceful and talented female line, and I no longer question the place I hold in my family. I look forward to passing on my legacy to my future daughter-to-be – and I'll make certain she cleans under the rim of the sink with a toothpick too.

The Exercise

- Make a list of concise memories and images of a family member, removed by more than one generation (grandparent, great aunt or uncle, great grandparent).

- Then, list your memories of a closer relative (sibling or parent).

- Then make a list of your own defining features, whether they be skills, talents or attributes.

- Make a web between the lists to point out similar themes and images.

- Write these lists as a poem.

For Those Who Wish to Sing, There is Always a Song[1] *Margot Van Sluytman*

Words (reading and writing) not only saved my life, they eventually gave me my life back. Hearing of an award I received from the US National Association for Poetry Therapy, for 'your work in facilitating growth experiences through experiential workshops in writing and healing voice', Glen Flett, the man who murdered my dad, contacted me. I chose to respond. We met. We shared hope and forgiveness in a ritual. My hurt and pain shifted profoundly, as did Glen's. Because of words, the murder of my father, Theodore Van Sluytman, was transformed from one devastating story of grief and horror, to a new story of hope and healing.

Always trust that no one can tell you how to feel. No one can enter your personal journey, your story, and your life. Your journey through healing is your own. I do not believe that any of us is exempt from raw savage pain. I do believe however that compassion for ourselves and for others leaves room for the beginnings of dialogue, challenging dialogue, with what it means to enter our life with a view to finding and or creating new normals that can in time include renewed hope. Words continue to nourish me and permit me the gift of sharing hope and possibility with others in my work with victims and offenders.

---

1   Swedish proverb.

I am filled with utter gratitude because the man who killed my father cares about what he did. His actions and words express that, and that matters to me. I believe that the encounter we have shared asks me to acknowledge how I might participate as a force of transformation, and reminds me that pen to the page and sharing my work with Expressive Writing with others, can and does bring about new and required paradigms. A deep sense of being supported continues to fill me. In sharing this short essay now, I feel supported. You are too. That we have choice to give and receive kindness and hope has been highlighted for me in knowing that life always asks us, as Gandhi said, to participate in being the change we wish to see. We can find the songs we need, we can in fact write them, we can read them, we can trust. And we need many, many songs. Many poems. Many dances with words.

How did writing allow me to see that I was more than murder, more than grief, more than mere mortal at the mercy of an unknown and unwanted deity? I began to read poetry. A simple act of choosing to find a way to navigate with metaphor, image, symbol, akin to the pictures, landscapes, and possibilities of the fairytales I loved so very much.

And then I trusted my pen to the page.

The Clock and Me *Nigel Gibbons*

Metaphor is part of the life blood of writing, and it can prove powerful to take a metaphor, extend it, send it out, then, almost magically, let it return, shedding light onto how we think and feel.

One dark, late winter afternoon, on the University of Bristol's Creative Writing for Therapeutic Purposes course, Rose Flint, one of our tutors, gave us Tess Gallagher's poem 'Black Silk' (Gallagher 1995, p.105) to look at, and Ruth Padel's observations on it (Padel 2007). In our reading we were asked to look at Gallagher's use of detail in the words she uses in describing the finding of a dead man's dress waistcoat. 'The poem does not describe him or the grief. He, and their grief, are internal. Grief happens on the inside of the words…' (Padel 2007, p.330).

The task was to write using an extended metaphor, to think of an object owned by someone we knew, and to allow the object itself to speak in our writing, whether poem or prose. If a key element of metaphor is 'the achievement of intimacy' (Hirsch 1999, p.15), then this exercise provided me with a safe, intimate space to express my feelings about the death of my father in 2004, and the survival of my mother, who had a stroke in 1999, and suffers from dementia.

I settled down, started writing, and before I was fully aware of what was happening, all sorts of memories had tumbled out. However, it took several drafts to arrive at a version I was happy to read out in class:

On the Occasion of your Marriage, 2 June 1956:
Albert Silvanus Gibbons

I was presented to you, to mark the start of your time
Together, man and wife, parents, grandparents,
Moving my hands I encircle your allotted span, you
Reliable, solid, dependable, always remembering
To wind, to set, day by day, winter to summer, summer to
     wintertime;
I remember your touch, never changing, always old
Never young, never fun, yet warm, caring; concerned,
To change my heart when it finally wore out, electrical
Instead of mechanical, battery not spring, silent instead of
     chime.
Your seasons turned, change of friends, job, house
But together, you were always together, until she was
Stroked by pain. You couldn't mend her broken mind,
Instead you took control, day by day, winter and summer,
She sat and watched, as you
Wore out your time, no one to wind you up, change your
     batteries, mend you;
When the time came, instead, lying there amidst the restless
     machines
You whispered, 'let me go', so you never came home
To change that winter to summertime, and nor can she, as she
Stares at my hands, slowly marking her lonely days,
Waiting.

One of the abiding memories I have of the house I grew up in is of a clock in our living room, presented to my parents 11 months before I was born. It had an inscription which I must have read hundreds of times. This close connection between the dates of the clock and my birth fascinated me: it existed in their lives before me, yet somehow I felt connected to it. Choosing the metaphor of the clock-given-to-them linked me back to my childhood, to the clock as a continuous presence in my parents' house which reflected me-as-given-to-them. In some ways it and I share a life.

Memories are important, they are an: 'essential part of ourselves' (Schneider and Killick 1998, p.37), and Andrea Gillies suggests that, 'It is memory that brings me to my life' (Gillies 2009). In writing the poem I stepped into my father's clock, I and the clock are speaking, sharing memories. It allowed me to articulate my own intimate thoughts about my father – these were some of the first words I wrote about him since he died – and it gave me space to separate myself from my feelings, whilst expressing them (Bolton 2006).

To me the poem suggests my father's dependability: he was reliable, gentle, precise. Yet there is also this sense of timelessness, a lack of change, an unending quality which ended when he died. However, as I re-drafted the poem I found that my feelings were more complicated. For instance, one of the earlier versions had a different ending:

> Then pain stroked her cheek and roles changed
> Hard working as always you wore yourself out,
> Accepting no help, tiring, your batteries failing
> No one there to change them for you, blood the precursor
> Of long weeks in between-ness, 'let me go' you whispered
> And eventually we did.

The focus in this earlier version was on his death rather than on my mother's survival, but it is her survival which has had a lasting impact on me. Her stroke was followed by dementia and she was unable to look after herself without my father, and so moved in to a flat in my house, changing many things for me and my family. There were changes for the clock too as it moved with her and sat alone and unnoticed. She rarely looked at it, because her concept of time changed as a result of her dementia. Similarly her relationship with me changed as I, to some extent, became my father for her, as her carer.

Kim Etherington describes how the act of forming our stories leads to an ordering of our experience, 'New selves form within us as we tell and re-tell our stories and when we write them down' (2004, p.9). The act of telling changes us. Writing the poem gave me the chance to tell my story, reflecting both on my father's death and the continuing legacy for me as carer for my mother.

The poem is not necessarily an accurate memory. Whilst I built the poem with my memories it's not how I felt at any particular moment in the past, but is interpreted through my present and past feelings, it's complicated (Schneider and Killick 1998).

Extending the metaphor as I wrote and re-wrote gave me the chance to understand a little of how I feel about my father's death and my mother's survival. It opened a door, offering me a chance to step in and explore further my reactions and feelings in all their simplicity and complexity.

Come In – to the Life of the Poem *Graham Hartill*

I wanted to write a poem to honour my father's life, and to help me come to terms with his death. But some time after I'd written the poem, it no longer seemed satisfactory – I'd written a poem *about* him, but not a poem with him *inside* it, not a poem *for* him. I'd like to explain what I mean by this, and how I put it right.

My father died of cancer with Alzheimer's, aged 77. He lived his entire life, apart from a spell in the army during the war, in the heart of the industrial West Midlands, where he worked as a coach builder. His private perfectionism and craftsmanship were given to his carpentry, spending weekends in the garden shed making furniture and doing odd jobs. He was a good man, who had no illusions that you had to work hard to get by; working day shifts and night shifts alternately, he was often exhausted by the simple necessity of providing for his family.

A few months after his death, I sat down in a Scottish arboretum to write my tribute. I approached the task with my eyes on history and topography: I was putting myself in a line of descent that stretched back, so I've since learned, through the same introverted place since the seventeenth century. My roots were the roots of industrial Britain. Looking back at it today, I'm struck how the opening of the poem also reflects the genesis of the poem itself:

> At first, little outcrops were quarried.
> Small industries developed.
> Coal began to be used instead of charcoal to smelt iron.
> Steam,
> canals, replacing packhorses.

The poem ended up nearly four pages long and a mixture of prose and verse, collaging historical material with thoughts about memory and memory loss, and blending images of blood, roses, steel, trees, wood and industrial fire. I was trying to work with the whole man, his origins, his place in the world at large, and was asking, implicitly, what identity is, especially that of a man whose sense of self was eroded by dementia. (My experiences of Dad's dementia became a fascination and a stimulus for my work with Alzheimer's patients in future years.) By paying tribute to his carpentry skills, I was also honouring the traditions of his class.

On a spiritual level the poem also embodies my Buddhist understanding of the transience of all phenomena, including memory:

> The fresh blood of the leaves that blow in his head. Gone now
> is the talking pain and the skull in document skin. No little
> jokes to make him smile, nor any recognitions.

And also present, inevitably, there is my obsession as poet with words themselves, my reflection on the ultimate impossibility of expressing the inexpressible, be it a life or a death. There is a passage about initials scratched in a local tree before the First World War, and the poem ends with a meditation on imaginary words writ large on a disused factory wall – for this is now the *post*-industrial age: I grew up in a dying world:

> We walk around in speech-marks,
> and there is no edge, to town or face, to claim
> > or fall from.
> As I type, the threat of demolition fades –
> > these lines are strewn across a disused factory wall,
> its light is lake-like, massive, and there is no weight.

It was published in an anthology (Chanan *et al.* 1989; later Hartill 2005), but this was not a poem I felt that confident to read out loud to others; I felt it a bit unwieldy, contradictory, lacking force. But a couple of years later I was running a workshop in Edinburgh and we were talking about family relationships. I found myself articulating a deeper problem with the poem that I hadn't been fully aware of: that Dad himself was in a way excluded from it: by his lack of education (he'd left school at 14 and hardly ever read anything but the paper), by his complete ignorance of poetry and, in my own mind, by my own high-falutin approach. In other words, he simply wouldn't have understood it. This was to me an unbearable irony.

Without compromising the poem itself, Dad had to be included on a deeper level, not just written about. The original poem was called 'For Tom', a name I never called him; now it was 'For My Father', honouring the true relationship. Then I wrote another piece as a direct address to him, and put it in the middle of the poem.

> Come into the circle, let me help you find the words, help you
> to spell...

Come into the circle – an invocation, actually inviting Dad into the creative process. Tell me – my father answers in the poem:

> I remember – men on buses, smoking Woodbines... Greece –
> that woman – standing in a doorway...

And I write about the woodwork that was close to Dad's heart in a direct, untrammelled way – this is a language he would understand, and sensual, physical, like the work itself. I'm trying to recreate the feelings and the satisfaction that was closest to his heart. In a way, this passage is as much his work as mine.

> Tell me, what was it like when you lifted the plane? It was
> heavy oblong lump of ash and steel. You'd lift it up by the
> shiny dark red well-palmed handle, your eyes steady above
> the vice, then swing it down. The oiled and certain blade
> would whisper the pine off in fragrant curls...

The Greeks had the notion of *apostrophe*: 'a figure of speech in which a thing, a place, an abstract quality, an idea, a dead or absent person, is addressed as if present and capable of understanding' (Cuddon 1976, p.53). Instead of just writing *about* my father as subject, I needed to invite him into the poem in person, and to ask him if he'd like to live there for a while. Perhaps, transfigured by death, anything was possible to him, even poetry, as long as he was welcomed into it.

My additions made the poem more projective, by which I mean that instead of being a passive thing, a poem *about* my father, it had now become more a poem *of* my father. A kind of use of my love for him had become an *expression* of it, the poem more of an action.

The process had helped me acknowledge something about the distance there had been between us, and helped me bridge it. I had fulfilled my task of paying tribute to my father; an act, which if honestly done, seems to me to be vital for any son, or daughter, to try to achieve.

Never Rub Out, Never Throw Away *Jonathan Knight*

My father owns a facsimile collection of John Constable's pencil drawings. Smaller than postcards, the early sketches of some of his most famous later oil paintings are fascinating to study. It is said that Constable never rubbed anything out and never threw any sketches away. They would be kept as a record of his artistic journey and provide ideas for future projects.

I admire Constable's discipline in preserving every sketch, no matter what the quality. The cut-and-paste and delete functions of my word processor mock my attempts to treasure the early drafts of a poem or short story. But occasionally I do review old pieces, dusting them off from the shoe box at the bottom of the wardrobe. Rereading something I have written, maybe after many years can be the trigger for a new writing project.

'Climbing Ben More' started life in 1993 as a short poem when I was still training in General Medical Practice. Reading it now, it appears simple and unsophisticated, much like the child's memories it contains. The poem only used the images of the climb without reflection or commentary.

Six years later, I was looking for a subject for a short piece to take to a creative writing workshop. Rereading the poem, I was struck by the metaphor of climbing with my father and learning the art of medicine, and wrote it, now as prose, reflecting on the newly found link.

I read the piece again recently, a few months after my mother died. The memory of that Scottish holiday is still vivid, and I now wonder whether there is more to explore in the simple story of a father and son climbing a mountain. During my mother's terminal illness my father, recently retired as a hospital doctor, took on the different role of care-giver and nurse. Now I saw the same diligence, gentle humour and quiet, uncomplaining approach that characterised his medical career as he looked after Mum. In this, too, he was teaching me how to approach the mountain climb.

If I hadn't kept the first, faltering attempt at writing about the climb, I may never have come to appreciate the influence my father has had on me. On mountain paths, you sometimes encounter cairns: piles of stones that mark the way on a difficult path to keep other travellers safe, or to mark the summit. Hill-walking tradition dictates that you add a stone to the cairn, becoming part of the landscape and helping preserve the ancient way-marker. Old pieces of writing are like cairns: mapping the routes we have travelled, and marking notable events that we might too easily forget. And like cairns, old writing can be added to and remodelled; in fact it may be essential to do so lest we get lost.

Climbing Ben More

Ben More was not our first mountain. Age one, I had dribbled down his neck as he had climbed Ben Nevis. My father has since delighted in reminding me that he needed to wrap my bib around his neck to prevent the rash from my saliva spreading. Ben More on the Isle of Mull, however, was my first proper mountain.

We had started early in the morning. The pattern was familiar. Never setting too fast a pace, but also trying to avoid too many stops, my parents became ever more inventive at trying to entertain my brother and myself, and distract us from sore feet and aching legs. Our favourite was the discovery of ginger nut bushes; the fruit of which were deposited by my father when we weren't looking from his secret supply. I was eight years old and understood the trick, but acted as surprised as my younger brother when another bush was found. I basked in the satisfaction of knowing the adult's secret whilst enjoying the child's mystery. Besides, I liked ginger nuts.

After lunch my mother and brother rested by a stream and my father and I pressed on. I can still see us walking together; the cold, damp air and our breath leaving its imprint hanging around our heads as if we were a pair of dragons marching towards our lair. The steep, narrow path, sometimes slippery, sometimes littered with rocks to test our concentration.

Most clearly of all, I remember my father's tales of previous expeditions when he was young. His impersonation of his eccentric Swiss guides who would call out in broken English to 'Don't Sleep!' (i.e. slip). The tubes of condensed milk, which they would squirt into their mouths as they walked along to avoid unnecessary delays.

He didn't force me to climb or set too fast a pace. He adjusted to me, and taught me how to climb. He shared the mountain with me. We fell into a rhythm of walking; zigzagging up the paths, taking smaller strides in the steepest sections. We took turns to lead, and stopped only occasionally to catch our breath and recheck our direction.

I learnt about mountains by climbing with my father, and I think I have learnt some of my medicine the same way. Here too, he has never forced the pace, but has shared the journey with me. There was the time he improvised an eye irrigation out of an egg cup. The fondness with which he referred to some of his patients (we loved the scatty elderly sisters nicknamed Hinge and Bracket), and the frustrations he had with needless bureaucracy. Clearest of all, I remember joining him on a ward round when I was eighteen. We moved methodically from bed to bed and ward to ward, taking care and time with each patient. I didn't yet understand the science of medicine, but I observed the craft, the steady rhythm and the art.

The most difficult part of our ascent of Ben More was the last twenty minutes. Slipping over cold, damp rocks, climbing through a clinging mist that wrapped itself around us, we pushed on for the summit. Then, suddenly, finding ourselves on the mountain top plateau, the mist fell away. Breathlessly we marvelled at our achievement, shared our last ginger biscuit, and laughed as we walked above the clouds.

CHAPTER 7

Relationships

Edited by Gillie Bolton

The authors of this chapter show how they used writing to gain insight and strength through bereavement or troubled times with loved ones. Penelope Shuttle tells us how once she refound poetry after her husband's death, it enabled her to 'articulate loss and grief' and begin to regain her active involvement in life. Australian poet, Les Murray, gives an account of how writing a poem about his experience of bullying in early relationships helped him overcome depressive illness.

Claire Williamson and Monica Suswin both used extended metaphors to help understand and cope with relationship breakdown. Interestingly Claire then uses a meta-metaphor: her cat is metaphor for the relationship; she then likens the cat to a handbag. This turning of abstract emotion to concrete object by metaphor is one of writing's illuminating gifts. Monica found using her metaphor later helpful with other problematic relationships. Both allowed their feelings to flow into their writing: trusting they would be safe, and insight would be engendered. Healing for Claire arose partly because her writing showed her repetitions and patterns, not only in her own actions, but in the behaviour of relatives and forbears. Monica explains how writing as if in dialogue with herself, calling herself *you* instead of *I*, helped her step outside her usual perceptions. She points out that sometimes pages of personal writing are required for illumination, whereas occasionally it happens in a few words (see also Munno 2006). Reinekke Lengelle uses a powerful method to draw strength and wisdom from her forbears. Terhikki Linnainmaa uses dream-like fiction writing to explore her relationship with herself.

Robert Hamberger wrote a gay love sonnet sequence through his partner's serious illness, finding the strict form a strong container for chaotic feelings, experiences and memories. Wendy French in Chapter 8 explains the opposite: how her poem about the chaos of loss had to be in a non-regular form; poetic form for her needing to follow content.

These authors emphasise the insight-generating power of redrafting. Robert finds reading his writing aloud to himself illuminating and helpful in the redrafting process; Monica Suswin also fruitfully reads and shares her writing with others. Robert glories in the playfulness of the sonnet-writing process. Monica suggests our mental processes are dramatic: 'the theatre of my mind'.

The Healing Fountain *Penelope Shuttle*

Time tends to get wobbly and smudged round the edges when you look back to a very difficult time.

But I'm pretty sure I didn't write anything in my husband Peter's last year or the year following his death. Things were just too hard; my unhappiness was too deep for me to draw comfort from reading or writing anything.

Virginia Woolf regarded mourning as a time when nothing happens or can happen, because one is simply imprisoned in time, frozen from any action.

But round about a year after Peter's death, there was a change, there was action. I'd closed the door on Peter's study bedroom after his death, and not set foot in his room since.

One day, without even thinking about it, I opened that door and went in. I suddenly found myself in there. I found no sense of his personality, just as there had been none anywhere in the house we'd lived in for almost 30 years when he died. He'd vanished. His room was simply a room. But now it was OK for me to be there.

On his desk was a folder of the fair-copy poems he had completed up to his death, put together in readiness for us to choose a new collection. But he'd been too ill to do so, of course.

I sat down, began to read his poems. And as I did, a door swung open. His last poems, rich, vigorous and inventive, full of life but written in the clear awareness of mortality and the afterlife brought poetry back into my life.

It was yet another of his gifts to me. He gave me back my life, changed by loss, but enriched now by poetry and by his love for and fascination with the world. He gave me back poetry, his last and lasting gift.

The very first poem of his I read that day was 'The Harper' (Redgrove 2006, p.42):

> the woman swimming
> At the heart of her harp,
> swimming in her evening clothes
> that make fresh signatures,
> Entering the music like Ophelia
> but a strong swimmer...

and this image of the woman, fully clothed, fully aware, swimming through the pool of life, immersed and capable in the waters of life, spoke to me deeply – that is why I called his posthumous collection *The Harper* (2006).

As I read Peter's marvellous last poems, I felt the dried-up well-springs of poetry and of life flow in me again, just as Denise Levertov describes in her poem 'The Well' (1967), where she writes of The Muse wading into deep and healing waters, and I began to write, to find words for grief, as Shakespeare advises us in *Macbeth*:

> Give sorrow words: the grief that does not speak
> Whispers the o'erfraught heart and bids it break...
> (Act IV, Scene III, lines 209–210)

As Seamus Heaney has pointed out, poetry can redeem the damage which loss inflicts on us. Poetry did indeed heal the damage I had sustained, depriving me of access of language and the imagination.

Once I was able to articulate loss and grief in the charged, flexible and blessed places language gives us, my stricken life was transformed into one of active and grounded involvement with the world, with family, friends, colleagues, students. Language is compassionate to our ills and hurts; W. H. Auden's 'healing fountain' (1979) is a reality, as is Ted Hughes' suggestion that in poetry we continue to talk to the people we have lost.

Burning Want *Les Murray*

Burning Want
From just on puberty, I lived in funeral:
mother dead of miscarriage, father trying to be dead,
we'd boil sweat-brown cloth; cows repossessed the garden.
Lovemaking brought death, was the unuttered principle.

I met a tall adopted girl some kids thought aloof,
but she was intelligent. Her poise of white-blonde hair
proved her no kin to the squat tanned couple who loved her.
Only now do I realise she was my first love.

But all my names were fat-names, at my new town school.
Between classes, kids did erocide: destruction of sexual morale.
Mass refusal of unasked love; that works. Boys cheered as seventeen-
year-old girls came on to me, then ran back whinnying ridicule.

The slender girl came up on holidays from the city
to my cousin's farm. She was friendly and sane.
Whispers giggled around us. A letter was written as from me
and she was there, in mid-term, instantly.

But I called people 'the humans' not knowing it was rage.
I learned things sidelong, taking my rifle for walks,

recited every scene of *From Here to Eternity*, burned paddocks
and soldiered back each Monday to that dawning Teen age.

She I admired, and almost relaxed from placating,
was gnawed by knowing what she came from, not who.
Showing off was my one social skill, oddly never with her
but I dissembled feelings, till mine were unknown to me too

and I couldn't add my want to her shortfall of wantedness.
I had forty more years, with one dear remission,
of a white paralysis: she's attracted it's not real nothing is
    enough
she's mistaken she'll die go now! she'll tell any minute she'll
    laugh –

Whether other hands reached out to Marion, or didn't,
at nineteen in her training ward she had a fatal accident
alone, at night, they said, with a lethal injection
and was spared from seeing what my school did to the world.
                                        (Murray 1998, p.446)

What did I get from writing my poem, 'Burning Want'? I'd tried to write
my depressive illness out of my system in the seven years (1988–95) since
it had come on, but only the addition of Marion's tragedy made it *work*.
That reminded me that depression can be a fatal illness. I also found that
a really truthful, accurately written record of events was indispensable –
you have to cast a clear light on piggy little neuroses, when you discover
their lairs, and you have to tell their stories over and over till even they,
who are very stupid, know they have been uncovered. Someone has said
a neurosis is a secret you don't know you're keeping! The poem initiated
a programme of accurate research, into my experience and what it could
show me. Stuff I'd known I knew, but had found it hard to express.
Nowadays, bullying is the stuff of half the TV series out of America,
but back when I'd served my time as a bit of a bush Asperger in a New
South Wales country town high school, there was no TV in Australia. I'd
got by with *From Here to Eternity*, an old movie you may have seen. I do
recommend it: it was my objective correlative, proof that others copped
it worse than I. Of course, I still had loads of probing and discovery to
do, about social patterns, family history, all the things that made me a

target, and not just me. Even the collective enforcement of political ideas, and why I refused all that with such loathing. But 'Burning Want' was a start, and gave me an instinctive relief the moment I completed it.

The events of 'Burning Want' run from 1951 to 1956. Or from my mother's death in 1951 from her third miscarriage to my departure to university in Sydney in 1957. I think most of the contents are self-explanatory, but I'll supply a few notes for orientation, then sum up the benefits I think the poem brought me, when I wrote it around 1995.

The people. Marion Grieg thought she was the daughter of the headmaster of the village school we both attended in 1952–3: a teacher left her file on her dad's desk and she found it, read it and discovered she was an adoptee. This shattered her world, and she was dead by suicide within five years. My mother had been a nurse: married in 1937, she had only one live birth, me, then a series of miscarriages that wrecked her morale and caused her to dislike me as their possible cause.

My dad was a timber getter whose idle father wanted him to fell a dangerous termite-ridden tree. When he refused, Granddad gave the job to his next younger son Archie, who had no timber skills and felled it into his skull, dying a few hours later. Granddad then set out to punish my father for this, by renting him a farm and keeping him poor, so that he could never be self-confident or have the wherewithal to escape. The farm was promised to him on Granddad's death, but of course that promise was broken too. Mum's death left my father a wreck for years, and my life was a Huckleberry one, not *all* bad, but gloomy near home. I'd also absorbed the atmosphere of sexual fear and disaster home was rife with, and my own little guilt as a possible matricide. I was too shy and naive for Marion, as was my cousin Peter Cornell whom she moved on to, and when I got to a pukka town school I copped a bad time from a cabal of girls – and gave them the edge of my vile tongue in return. All bad magic for future relations with womenfolk.

Blast, I meant to be brief in this background note, and I see I've failed. But perhaps the human fixes we were all in are relevant and essential. The motives of the girls who went for me I've never discovered. 'We were only 16', one of them said to me years later when she was dying of cancer. She's the only one of them I ever saw again, when we reached 17 and went our ways. What did I say back to her? I confess I grinned and replied, '*I* was only 16', and then we both let the matter drop, there in the cancer ward.

Leaving Tortilla, My Cat *Claire Williamson*

I pick her up
with no resistance
and like a badly packed
mink handbag
she falls into two halves of cat
around her skinny middle.

This is what it is to hold my baby
the baby that I feel
I cannot take with me

like my mother before me.
When all the boxes are stacked
the books are packed
the bags filled to bursting

there will be one bundle
remaining in the living room
staring numbly at the ceiling

or simply sleeping through
the leaving.

This poem explored unresolved feelings about leaving my husband, but also my cats. When I left my marital home, my actions were compulsive. Later, I looked back and wondered at what had driven me to such an extreme act. I began writing it as I sat in a café, waiting for my friend Sara. I always write by pen, in my portable journal.

'Tortilla' was my little black cat. Tortilla carried a lot of projections during the relationship and was often used to communicate difficult things, for example, 'Tortilla says you forgot to lock the door.'

Sat in the café writing, I was aware that I'd forgotten my purse and knew I'd have to ask Sara to pay for lunch; a rare moment of dependency for me. Sara has also been a mother-figure in my life and this was a real opportunity fully to receive something from her. Being open to receiving love has been a struggle throughout my life. This writing context feels important with regard to the poem. As a child, I would have been totally dependent on my mother, just as Tortilla was dependent on me.

My own mother left me with my father when I was one year old. She committed suicide six years later.

As I wrote the poem, I was transferring my own childhood feelings onto Tortilla. She becomes a metaphor for myself as a baby. Interestingly, the roots of the words 'transference' and metaphor are the same. Clarkson makes the case for transference:

> The etymological roots of the Greek and Latin words for transference mean 'to carry across', so there is a sense of movement from one place to another.
>
> (Clarkson 2008, p.69)

and Padel provides a beautiful definition for metaphor:

> Greek roads used to be full of little three-wheeled vans with METAPHORS written, in Greek, on the front. I once asked the driver of one what his job was. 'Taking something', he said, 'from one place to another.' This is also the classic definition, Aristotle's definition, of metaphor.
>
> (Padel 2007, p.34)

This poem, 'Leaving Tortilla' brought insightful movement within me. I began with the image of picking up Tortilla, remembering the way that all her weight would fall away from her middle, almost as if she was dead. At this point in the poem, it isn't clear whether the cat is dead, or not. 'Leaving Tortilla' marks an ending of our relationship, there is a sense of death. As Clarkson simply states:

> The existential reality is that endings are part of life. Death is about ending... We live in the presence of our mortality and the avoidance of death detracts from the vitality of our lives... Each ending is a fractal of other endings both historically and in the future.
>
> (Clarkson 2008, p.171)

To continue the metaphor of Tortilla as myself as a child, I believe that when my mother left, I experienced a spiritual death of sorts. In the poem I can see clearly that leaving my husband and the cats was repeating what my mother had done to our family. However, I am also sure of my love for Tortilla, which has helped me to understand that my mother's departure was not my fault and that she loved me deeply.

I have found Family Constellations, developed by Bert Hellinger (www.hellinger.com), useful in understanding the concept of patterns that repeat through generations. In Family Constellations an 'entanglement' is where one family member follows the fate of an earlier family member. Families that have experienced trauma can stop acknowledging a particular member, due to the emotional fallout of the trauma. Family Constellations are a way of bringing the unacknowledged family member back into people's thoughts and to allow the original trauma to be witnessed, opening up the potential for healing.

My mother's suicide was traumatic and challenging for my family. Whatever she was acting out by leaving, felt unresolved; just as understanding why I left my husband felt unresolved for me.

The journey to unpick the repeating pattern is in progress; I am working with my mother's family to bring her back into consciousness. I am in a relationship, and although I still have compulsions to leave, I can stay with the feelings, rather than acting on them.

But, I did leave Tortilla, like my child-self, not dead, but quite amazingly alive with all that purring. The grief was somatised: hence the numbness or sleep, saved for a later date when it can be acted out or understood. In the poem, Tortilla becomes the 'badly packed bag' that I could have used to describe myself, and have subsequently written about in an uncrafted list:

The Badly Packed Bag
Jammed in; crammed down.
Pieces hanging out.
Open to stealing.
Raw to the elements.
Overfull.
Unzipped.
Bulging in the wrong places; lumpen.
Abandoned.
Unloved.
Untidy.
Things get lost.
Carrying the baggage, whilst trying to stay true.

I have been able to use this 'spin-off' poem to help myself with very simple personal habits: leaving myself open to hurt, reflecting on recurring feelings of abandonment, letting feelings out in a manageable way and even negative eating habits.

I believe that all poems, and even raw splurges, are important; always moving towards more insight; always on the way to healing and integration.

Wall Writing *Monica Suswin*

> You are a wall of crumbling bricks; each one compacted rubble, one on top of the other. The sheer force of all that compressed rubble keeps this towering structure in place. My wall to meet *you* is a steel wall. You can kick it as much as you like, dent it, bash it, if you get too close all you will see is yourself – yes, someone riding full pelt on a steamroller.
>
> (Journal extract, Winter 2006)

This is angry writing, addressed to Hilda (not her real name). The feelings flying around between us were such that after several unsuccessful attempts to discuss the issues, I was too angry to speak. She did not or could not understand my point of view.

My purpose is to explain how this writing helped me deal with myself after I was unable to handle the matter in 'real life'. So it doesn't really matter who Hilda is or what we were arguing about. When I can't express my feelings they have nowhere to go, so they tend to implode. When my emotions intensify I write to sort out my turmoil, and my inner life usually settles down. I was desperate for the anger to go away and leave me in peace.

I was furious with Hilda because I believed she misrepresented my views. I still ask myself whether I might have been better off venting this anger more directly. I don't know the answer. Being angry is a normal response to not being heard. I decided I would write about two walls which represented something about the quality of our relationship: the crumbling bricks for her, the steel wall for me.

Using my imagination in this way lets me play with language and ideas. I find that a solid thing, a vividly described three-dimensional object, brings an innovative quality to feelings I would rather not have. In fact, a fresh energy was brought to bear on this intransigent situation. With these few sentences I have transformed and explored the abstract quality of hostility into a nameable-thing allowing the job of the metaphor to do its amazing work.

Metaphor is rather wonderful. In his poem 'The Thought Fox', Ted Hughes uses a fox as a metaphor for his own inspiration captured on the page, as well as the spirit of the creature he has also caught: 'in some ways my fox is better than an ordinary fox. It will live for ever. And all through imagining it clearly enough and finding the living words' (1967, p.21). I found out the purpose of my own wall, by describing its function as I explored the metaphor.

Instead of the familiar 'I' voice, I also stepped outside my normal perceptions by addressing myself in the second person. This is what I wrote:

> There is an edge to your wall and there you may conduct
> your meetings.
> The wall allows the meeting between you and the other.
> (Journal extract, Summer 2006)

How did I write about these two walls? I thought of Hilda and invited a wall to be built in my mind's eye, and then I did the same for myself. This expressed our conflicting roles in this dramatic scenario – the theatre of my mind.

I described the wall as accurately as I could; usually as I write the image becomes clearer and might change in detail. Visualising all that compacted and compressed rubble made me wonder whether there might be a vulnerability trapped within this towering structure. Could this be the nature of Hilda's defence system masking a hidden hurt? All I'd been aware of was someone steamrollering me with their own anger, hence the shift to imagining her hitting out at the steel wall. It makes sense that my wall would be one of steel as I closed off my emotional responses.

The exploration of my feelings through the writing helped me understand Hilda a little better from my own perspective. I could not be sure of my conclusions as we were unable to have a satisfactory conversation. I found a little compassion, and so my anger shifted to some extent. I say to some extent because the problem was neither solved nor possible to resolve. But putting my energy into the writing stopped me discussing the issues any further.

I always read aloud to myself, sometimes repeatedly: either an indication of extreme satisfaction or that I haven't got it quite right. I may read my piece to someone else: this brings a different reality and connection to the original unsatisfactory event. Of course I would never have read this to Hilda. I wrote the paragraph above straight onto my computer screen with no redrafting. It is a tiny extract from pages and pages of writing, however.

Three years later the image of the two walls still holds a certain power. Within the context of my relationships I have used this extended metaphor of the wall many times. It has been instructive in helping me understand myself and my friends better. Real walls are about divisions of space in a building, or a statement of ownership around a garden or territory. The imaginative pattern of my own boundary as a human being shifts with different people, depending whether I feel close or distant, self-protective, or open armed.

Hilda and I are still in contact; the issue is over and done with, and I am no longer angry with her nor she with me. But the writing told me a truth: of that I am sure. The beauty of the metaphor means I am able to use the same image many times for all sorts of moods and circumstances. Explorations of this nature are endless and exciting, as I never cease to be surprised and exhilarated by the power the writing holds for me.

Invoking the Ancestors *Reinekke Lengelle*

I use written dialogues to evoke (or invoke) my ancestors in written dialogues. I imagine they have wisdom for me and I call on them to assist me when I feel stuck or in pain. Here is how I started writing in this way.

Several years ago we bought land in a town in the Rocky Mountains. We borrowed against our home, rather aware that mortgage translates as 'death pledge'. This was the first major financial risk my husband and I had taken and we were nervous. A year later we borrowed even more and built a cabin. Today a beautiful red-roofed home with two bedrooms, a vaulted ceiling, and a wood-burning fireplace stands as proof of our efforts.

While doing dishes one afternoon at home in the city, I wondered if we had made a good decision. I couldn't pretend that we could change our minds, but hoped for some reassurance. I thought of Bert Hellinger, founder of Family Constellations' work (1998, 2001; Ulsamer 2005), and his perspective on the role of ancestors. In a group exercise, a facilitator may invite a participant to stand in front of a row of ancestors (represented by others in the group) in order to feel their strength. These family members were obviously strong enough to survive generation after generation which resulted in the individual's own birth. As I stood by the sink, I spontaneously saw the image of my mother's parents standing behind me.

My maternal grandparents had renovated old farm houses in the Netherlands, in their forties and fifties. They also made frequent trips to the Swiss Alps on a tight budget in their Volkswagen Beetle, with their three daughters. They had survived the war; my grandfather in a concentration camp, my grandmother almost starving with my toddler mother in Amsterdam. When I was a child they visited Canada and travelled with us to the Rocky Mountains and if they were alive now to see our cabin, I know they would have cheered us on and toasted us, eager to share the joy. They would also have waved away any concerns about our newly acquired bank loan. Since the day I imagined their support, I haven't worried about the debt.

In order to write a dialogue with my ancestors, it's important I feel I am 'embodying' each voice and listen for what feels true.

Example

Journal notes: I have some questions about which direction my work should take. More teaching? More writing and less teaching? Is my book project doable at this stage?

I decided to invoke my grandfather Ber. When he died he left me his books which were about things like the archetypal meanings of fairytales and contained all kinds of philosophical and esoteric wisdom. He told me the meaning of life was simply to live it. He used to serve me tea at 92; he could barely see then.

R: It looks like I'm supposed to be teaching less, just now.

Ber: Finally, you let me speak! My goodness, I have really been waiting for you to call on me. What took you so long Alice? (His pet name for me was Alice – from *Alice in Wonderland*.)

R: I've been rather busy, as you know.

Ber: Yes, busy, busy, busy. And forgetting presence. You need to empty out at least half your files and get *rid* of some books. Your office is too full. You have a lot of work ahead of you. This is the little bit of peace you're going to have before getting down to business.

R: I'm afraid all that hard work is going to take the soul out of the work.

Ber: No, the busy-ness takes the soul out of work, not the hard work. The lack of presence takes the soul out of work. Be where you are. The simplest and hardest thing to do. (*He starts to snicker in his pseudo-evil way.*)

R: What's the season for me and my work?

Ber: Your energy is going to the roots again. To the root country for one and to the root of you. You went through a cycle of blossoming, all your energy was beautifully flowering on the outside branches. What a show it was! Now you're going into fall and winter. You have to rest, but in a deliberate way. The time you're being given is crucial. Stay close to your own source. Refuel slowly and choose carefully.

R: What do you think of this book I'll be writing?

Ber: You've put yourself up to the task because you want to mature in the work. It's good use of your energies, but first 'put your house in order'.

R: Today the words that came to mind were: you have to become a student again.

Ber: A humble position. Yes. It's very fair to say that.

R: I notice a bit of shame around that.

Ber: You know it's a good place to be, too. You have to go like the water, to the lowest place. (*Another snicker.*) Just last week you said, water has two choices, to flow up or down…ha! Now the joke is on you.

R: OK. I get it. Thank you. It's good to hear from you.

After writing a dialogue like this one, I realise that I could just be 'making it up' or that it's only one perspective on a given situation. However, I'm often struck by how useful it is to hash out something like this with someone you feel supports you, even if only in spirit.

In this particular dialogue, I also noticed that I enjoyed my grandfather snickering at me in his familiar, loving way.

A Dreamlike Story of Imagination *Terhikki Linnainmaa*

I wanted to try writing fiction, but for years I had written factual text and no fiction since school days, and this bothered me. I pictured a dream-like story inspired by a 'road movie', imagining the story's various phases. I thought about the sensory perceptions connected with them one at a time: smells, colours, sounds, movements, textures and temperatures. At a Gillie Bolton workshop in Lahti, Finland, May 2008, having written about a childhood incident, I received a revelation: dreams, memories and stories bubble up from the same source, the unconscious. I was doing what I had heard Fritz Perls once said: 'Lose your sense and come to your senses.'

> *I desire you*
> My heart begins to pound as I get near you. I feel my breath coming faster. I want to caress your shining outer shell, which glistens in the sun with its waxed finish, but I am afraid of leaving fingerprints on your surface. I step onto your running board and with trembling hands open the door using the chrome handle. From inside the scent of old leather wafts into my nostrils. The scent reminds me of car trips with Him, a wicker picnic basket and red and white chequered linens.

Now everything is different. We leave on a journey of escape with you. I have dressed myself in a red flowered chiffon dress and a wide brimmed summer hat. You like them, I know that. I glance behind us: no, no one is following us. I open the window; the breeze cools my fevered cheeks. I could open the white top completely, driving like Isadora long ago. What a way to die! I could die in your arms!

With trembling hands I start you. You cough quietly. I sink into your front seat as if in a safe lap. Your V-engine purrs evenly. I take a worried glance behind: are we being followed? I see nothing but a cloud of dust. My fear is eased somewhat but my heart is still racing. We are passed by a BMW that appears out of nowhere. The young blonde driver smirks at me remarkably. I don't let it bother me very long; behind your heavy nose I feel safe.

I turn onto a narrow side road. The sea shore blinks from the shade of leafy trees. The wind brings the scent of salt. I see a wooden dock, on each side boats gently rock in the waves. I want to take a walk to calm myself. I park you on the shore. My black patent leather high heeled shoes tap as I walk along the dock. A middle-aged couple both grey haired and tanned, load beer cases into a fisherman-style boat. 'The girl has a really old Packard,' the man says. I smile quietly; I don't want to say anything about myself or you, especially about our journey of escape.

Suddenly, from far away, I hear a car. I am frightened; a cold sweat rises on my forehead: what if it is Him… I try to get back to your safe lap quickly. In my rush my heel catches, my shoe comes off; I almost fall. I push my shoe back. The man watches my escape in wonder, his look only increases my fear. I get back to you and we continue our journey, you and me. Behind us can only be seen a cloud of dust. I sigh with relief.

I do not interpret using universal symbols. Every element of a dream or fictional story (person, building, plant, means of transportation, what ever) represents myself. There are several possibilities which of the

elements in the preceding story could represent me. I can best identify
with the people in the story, the young woman as well as the older
couple. This story has the same types of longing and admiration for
freedom as found in 'road movies' which I have liked.

Gillie Bolton said novelist Lesley Glaister found her unusual
characters 'from within myself, thus they all have to be me' (Bolton
1999, p.111). Bolton said fiction writing can be a lot of fun. Since it
is creative: I can let my imagination take flight, write whatever I want.
Through fiction we can try things which are impossible in real life. Tales
of imagination are roads which are not travelled in life. Stories can have
disturbing elements but they are not inevitable. My own story contains
fear and threats from which we escape with the help of a secure character.

The 'red line' in my story is security, represented by the big, heavy
car. The conflicting elements are the flight to freedom and security.
These elements were very important for me at the time of writing. I
was tied down by various responsibilities and therefore my dream was
for some kind of get-away, even a temporary one. On the other hand
security has always been important for me.

A Heart-shadow Fell at Our Feet: Writing a
Sequence of Love Sonnets *Robert Hamberger*

I have no idea how the idea first occurred to me. I'd recently finished one
love sonnet to my partner Keith, called 'Walking Together', written after
we saw a traffic light shining ahead at night:

> It glowed at the crest of an avenue of trees
> still young and green, while a heart-shadow fell
> at our feet from a streetlamp through leaves.
>
> (Hamberger 2002, p.75)

Another sonnet began a couple of weeks after that: 'Two Men Together',
this time about us chatting as we prepared for bed one night. Its
undercurrent was whether we would or wouldn't out ourselves to the
neighbours as two gay men living together, although I now imagine our
neighbours knew exactly what we were.

The idea clicked of trying to write a diary of love sonnets, perhaps ten or so, once these poems were drafted. I thought I'd try to include all the excitement, pleasures, history and routines of any love affair between any couple, whatever their sexuality. An erotic sonnet 'Each Other's Skin' was started soon afterwards, and the sequence began to find its own shape.

I have always written autobiographical poems, and use the writing process to explain my experience to myself. If they make any sense to, or connect with, other readers, that's an unexpected bonus. During the drafting process (and by reading back to myself the product of juggling rhymes, rhythms and images) I begin to understand what I feel about an experience. It's often a surprising recognition.

Then life intervened. Six weeks after the first sonnet threw its heart-shadow image, Keith was unexpectedly admitted to hospital with heart problems. Sub-acute bacterial endocarditis, which I read in the medical dictionary had a 10–30 per cent mortality rate.

So the routines of this particular couple changed dramatically. What choice did I have but to reflect those changes in my diary of love sonnets?

I now believe that those first sonnets, written before Keith's illness interrupted us, involved not only a premonition of the months ahead, but came at a perfect time to protect me, to say *Here is this sonnet form that has helped to give you a structure in previous difficult times. Here, now, is the subject you didn't choose, but which you must write about, to help you through this experience.*

For the five weeks when Keith was having intravenous antibiotics and discussions about heart surgery, there's no doubt that writing kept me company. My journal was full of fear and love, alongside new routines of balancing daily hospital visits, my job and regular contact with my children 140 miles away. I was able to channel this chaos into the reliable order of sonnets, which still included fear and hospitals, but also a voice talking to itself as honestly as possible.

'Diagnosis' was written immediately after Keith's hospital admission:

From the foot of your hospital bed the doctor
described your heart: its infection, its leaky valve,
surgery in a few months to solve
the problem. We needed some air
and discovered a garden with a slow fan of water

drowning geraniums. You said 'How instructive
this is!' We kept quiet a while to give
ourselves a breather, next year
already mapped out for us: a line
of stitches down your chest, taking it easy,
a slow recovery. Is this the heart's infection,
this need to keep less than a beat away
from each other whatever might happen?
I watched wet leaves. You watched the water sway.

                                    (Hamberger 2002, p.63)

That poem correctly predicted the year ahead: the wait before surgery; meeting the surgeon; before the operation; Keith's time in intensive care; his return home. The diary of our love continued taking shape, until 18 months later 21 love sonnets had been completed. I then re-shuffled them to make narrative sense to readers, give them a 'story' about this unknown couple. That re-ordering led to 'Walking Together' (the first poem to be written) ending the sequence in the published version, as if the heart-shadow had become a conclusion rather than a starting-point.

I have a history of enjoying writing sonnets and sequences, although all the sequences I've previously written had either been free-verse or alternated free-verse with sonnets. After deciding that I would set myself the deliberate challenge of writing a sonnet sequence, I knew I would learn from the masters and mistresses, and attempt to mould that wonderful tradition to fit my voice (see Paterson 1999). Although many of Shakespeare's sonnets are addressed to a man, part of my experiment was to subvert that tradition for an explicitly gay context: to explore issues of safety and danger relevant to any gay couple, alongside the obvious celebration of our relationship.

How did writing these poems help me? Playing with words, shaping lines into end-rhymes in a sonnet's pattern 21 times, served both as a distraction from what was happening to Keith and an opportunity to focus on what was happening to *me* during his illness. It became a chance to play, in a serious fashion, and to use that play-time as a prism to focus as closely, almost as clinically, as possible on the range and contradictions of my reactions.

One aim was to explore whether I might find a thread of meaning through the incoherent mess of my feelings: take a line through the labyrinth and see if I could feel my way back. If I could make sense of it, there was a possibility (a hope, through the writing process) that I might even end up with lines that created some beauty from the mess: my version of the truth about my experience of Keith's illness (since I could only guess at his experience). All love poems trumpet the poet's feelings, using the loved one as notes to play those feelings. *This is how I write when I'm in love. These are the words I find when I might lose the man I love.*

The sonnet's pre-ordained template lends reassurance during writing: I *will* find a shape for my experience and it will become a sonnet's shape. So any therapeutic benefit is both via absorption in the process (a way of hearing myself) and delight in finding a path through each sonnet's maze of 14 lines: achieved; making sense; trying yet again – with whatever words come to hand – to discover my self.

—◆◦●◦◆—

CHAPTER 8

Personal Loss

Edited by Gillie Bolton

Loss is one of the hardest things we have to bear. We lose in so many ways: loved ones, health, career, objects, dignity, hope. These authors show us how writing can temper pain, and become eulogy or celebration of the lost. Wendy French writes of a triple loss, the lost object standing as extended metaphor for the two others; an ancient poem fragment by Sappho inspired her. She felt in this poem that free verse was the form she needed to express and explore her chaotic feelings, form needing to mirror content (the opposite of Robert Hamberger's use of sonnet, see Chapter 7). Sarah Birnbach tells us about journal freewriting; the journal being a container, or safe space to explore and come to terms with events and feelings, and an ever-present friend to whom she can express anything. Yvonne Watson also used freewriting to express and explore anger, denial, guilt, and to help her find comradeship in the universality of grief and bereavement.

Writing in the voice of an unknown person depicted in a picture or postcard was a workshop exercise Deborah Buchan found illuminating. She wrote unsent letters in the form of free verse from this character, finding fiction offered distance and safety. She found sharing her writing with a trusted facilitated group, enabled her grieving to begin and further integration of feelings to take place, as did Leone Ridsdale who also discussed her writing with family. Leone Ridsdale also gained inspiration from published prose, fiction and poetry. Joanne Robinson describes how completing sentence stems suggested by a facilitator helped illuminate her loss. A painter, she discovered that writing enabled meaningful reflection on her non-verbal creative work.

To a Gold Ear-ring, Head of Nefertiti *Wendy French*

I conversed with you in a dream
(Sappho [trans. Carson 2002, p.273])

What I had is lost.
I cannot look at you exactly
but I can talk to you

and I can see and see again
your silted head listening by my ear.
There were two of you – whether in flight

or fall – one has disappeared.
I've heard echoes from the past;
how you grew into me, became a part of sleep.

Fourteen years of a straightening,
branching out and while the planet
slowly disappears

you will become gold-dust. Ground.
My other ear-ring, carefully removed sits
in a stained glass bowl which reflects my naked face.

This poem was written after a fallow period of just waiting for words/phrases to begin to form in my head. I had had a year of tragedy and life changes. I was unable to write anything remotely creative that could begin to have meaning for someone other than myself. People encouraged me by saying that this didn't matter at this stage in my life. I just needed to write whatever came in to my head. This form of outpouring served me well for about six months and then I became increasingly frustrated with myself and my work. In the same year that my beloved niece was killed in a tragic accident while cycling for a greener London my son left London to go and live abroad. While he still had his life ahead of him my niece had lost hers but I knew I was no longer going to be an everyday relevant person in Tom's life.

Two things happened to make me feel I could express myself again. I was introduced to Ann Carson's translation of Sappho's fragments, 'If Not, Winter'. These fragments and this translation enthralled me. The space that the reader is given around each fragment allows for individual interpretations of the meaning of the fragment and indeed, in turn, this allows space to begin the process of writing again. I became excited by reading once more.

At the same time as this awareness of the 'self on and off the page' and my personal need for space in order even to think about being able to write again, I lost an ear-ring: one of a pair that I had worn for 14 years. The ear-rings were tiny and in the shape of the head of Nefertiti. They had been a present from my son after a school exchange holiday abroad when he was away from home for the first time on his own. They represented independence, a growing away, the loss of a child into adolescence, and my own middle age. I had worn them every day for 14 years until one fell away. The loss of this ear-ring became far more significant than the mere fact of it being lost. It felt like the sudden cutting of the umbilical cord. The feelings were totally irrational. Objects are lost every day. The ear-rings would not have had any monetary value. One night I dreamt I was talking to the ear-ring, telling it to come home and that's when I knew I had to write a poem about it. In the same dream the head of my niece, Rachael, appeared and told me life still has to be run. The epigraph to Sappho allowed me in, 'I conversed with you in a dream.'

The opening line is deliberately short and stark. The truth of loss had to be addressed. The ear-ring, my son as he was, and Rachael, all will never return. The son and the ear-ring become intertwined, one standing for the other. In the past, my son would have listened to me and the ear-ring was constantly by my ear. The head of Nefertiti and Rachael were synonymous. Then everyone goes their own ways, my son into adulthood, Rachael into death and the ear-ring into the ground. I imagined the ear-ring being trodden down by a stranger and becoming part of the earth. The other ear-ring sits in a glass-mirrored box and when you look into it, it seems that the past is reflected back and with increasing age, exposure.

The first stanza of this poem set the rhythm, the intonation, the sounds, the syntax; the poem would not have worked if it had been written in a regular form. The form and content of this poem had to reflect each other. The loss here was chaotic; the form had to curb my chaos, pull it to order so that I could make something meaningful out of something meaningless. I missed the dangling feeling of the ear-rings swaying whichever way my head turned and so to have written the poem in a particular form would have been misjudged for this poem. The left hemisphere of the brain controls language and the right hemisphere controls synthetic and holistic operations, especially those involving images, metaphor and music. So to create a poem we have language competing with order. This in itself was insightful and helped me to write the poem. Some time earlier a young girl I had been working with had committed suicide. I felt compelled to write about her as we had had a close relationship as client and therapist. However words spilled out all over the page and I could make nothing meaningful out of words and her senseless death. It was only when I tried the poem in the pantoum form that the strict rules helped the poem to take shape. For me, in my professional role, I had been unable to keep the young girl safe. I needed to rein in my emotions and take control. Rachael's death, my son growing up and the ear-ring were losses out of my control. It was only after I'd written this poem that I realised how the ear-ring had become my son and also Rachael and how the three losses were so intertwined that together they could create a whole in the form of a poem.

Writing this poem helped me to understand what was going on in my life and how I had to get back into control again. To write the poem was emotionally healing. The pain of loss does not go away or diminish but it changes and once I had found again the ability to put pen to paper I could begin to think about the next stage of living. I now understand that loss is not just about grieving for and tackling the more obvious losses in life – death, divorce, illness, etc., but that writing about more insignificant losses (the loss of an ear-ring for example) therapeutically led me to a greater examination of what was happening at this particular time. I now know that when words have left me I need to read Sappho's fragments to aid my writing process.

The Final 'Good Bye'   *Sarah Birnbach*

For over 25 years, journaling has given me the kind of emotional sustenance that eating and sleeping have provided to my physical wellbeing. Freewriting – the 'unstructured, free-form narrative writing that starts anywhere and goes where it pleases' (Adams 1993, p.51) – has been my primary journaling process for most of these years; though many further journaling techniques are available (see for example Adams 1993).

My journal was my safe haven – the place to express my emotions in an uncontained and unrestrained way during the nine days preceding my father's death, as he lay unconscious in intensive care. Freewriting, so perfect for the free flow of uncensored thoughts and emotions, allowed me to speak the unspeakable and reflect my soul's experience.

My father entered the hospital for an angiogram and immediately underwent unanticipated double bypass heart surgery on 11 September 2000. For the next nine days, I witnessed the life ebb from my father's body as he gradually left this world.

My journal became the container for my fears and anxieties – the friend I turned to when life outside the small depressing waiting room became more than I could bear. That time spread as an expanse between the brief, limited visiting hours.

> September 13: There's no recognition of me or Mom at all. Not a flicker of his eyelids. Not a quiver of his lips. No pressure from his fingertips. I think of the song, Papa can you hear me…? The absence of an answer is deafening in its silence.

> September 15, 4:10 pm: How do I ready myself to lose him? How do I stay strong? If Dad knows that we are all here – will he know he's dying? Do I tell him to fight? Or let go? The fear and conflict are overwhelming. I'm certain he wouldn't want us to keep him like this! But I'm not ready to say 'good bye'.

> September 15, 8:20 pm: I'm lost… like being in a ship without a rudder. It is now four full days since his surgery and Daddy's not rallying. The doctor says: 'Be optimistic.' But I feel like I'm witnessing him being washed out to sea and I'm

powerless to do anything to save him. Please, God, let him go in peace. I don't want to lose Daddy, but this is becoming torturous; I am trying, trying, trying to be patient. It is getting harder and harder and harder…

September 16, 11:30 am: It is so hard to sort out all the feelings. They come and go like the waves of the ocean. The sadness overwhelms and recedes. Numbness comes in and recedes. Fatigue comes in and recedes. Optimism hardly comes in any more.

September 17, 5:25 pm: I'm trying to feel strong when Mom feels overwhelmed. When she said 'I don't know how I'll live without him', she gave words to the fear that's living deep in the darkest corners of my heart.

September 18, 11:30 am: It's gut wrenching to watch other patients come into ICU, recover and leave. And Daddy is still lying there. This man, who has always been so private, is lying exposed for everyone to see. Janie has spoken the unspeakable: 'We should start to let him go.' As soon as she said that, all pretenses of control evaporated and I let go and sobbed uncontrollably in her embrace.

September 18, 5:45 pm: I am alone with Mom and my fears and you, my dear journal. The medical professionals say it's grave, but they've seen people in this situation who have turned around before. They have not given up hope…why have I? I hate to see him like this. I HATE IT! I HATE IT! I HATE IT! I HATE IT!

September 19: The doctors appear so briefly…they are in and gone like a shooting star. I crave their input…any input. It's better than the cavernous vacuum of unknowing. But when they speak, it's a foreign language to my ears: creatinine levels, hemodynamic, blood ureanitrogen, hyperalimentation. When did my father become a subject for this vocabulary? Why do the doctors talk as if my father were an inanimate object? Has he become no more than his vital signs and bodily functions?

There is no journal entry on 20 September 2000. Emotional grief work was postponed until the practical necessities were handled. Standing beside my father as he died, numbness overtook my body and soul. On 21 September, my first journal entry became my eulogy to my father.

My journaling steadied me during those last days of my father's life. My writing process provided the freedom to express my tumultuous emotions, which, in turn, gave me strength when I needed strength the most in that lonely place in time. As gruelling as the internal struggle was, confronting it in my journal was safer than speaking the words out loud. Processing my feelings in my journal for those nine days helped prepare me for the final moments of my father's life and for the final 'good bye'.

Something We Need to Learn to Live Alongside
Yvonne Watson

This poem came about after the tragic loss of two close friends who had been at my wedding and were god-parents to my children. They were committed Christians who lived their beliefs in the best possible way by offering their service to the community alongside working full time. I suppose what I am trying to say is that they were people who made a difference and who would be hugely missed by all their family and friends.

My personal therapist suggested I write something to help cope with my grief immediately following this loss. I was appalled by this idea – in retrospect I think this was part of the 'denial' that surfaced throughout the grieving: to put words onto paper would mean the loss was real. Although I knew it was 'real' my words and thoughts were often 'I can't believe it.'

I felt that I did want or need to write something, some months later – but what I wanted was to write something shocking and violent. I wrote these poems in my head only. For some reason I could not put words on paper; nothing could do justice to the strength of my shock and sadness.

It was then that I realised how angry I was – how furious at the perpetrator and how furious at the people I had lost – why hadn't they left on their journey five minutes later? Why had they been out at all? Didn't they know they were needed?

That is an anger that alongside denial still rolls through my emotions like distant thunder. Yet I did not want to write an angry poem. I knew that those Christian people would be forgiving and that to do justice to their memory would not involve furious violent images on paper.

My responses to the suggestion of writing, first the refusal to contemplate it and then the quite scary feeling of wanting to create a really shocking image on the page, helped me to understand what I was actually experiencing emotionally. These feelings were buried under the generalised shock and sadness.

The poem I wanted to write started to surface some time later again. I find most of my writing begins with an emotion or an idea that somehow seems to form of its own accord and appears most frequently first thing in the morning. Then I freewrite, and later shape the words into something like a poem. I allowed words to fall onto the page before I began to think about them or their effect.

The poem was redrafted many times – I wanted it to be cathartic. For it to have this healing effect meant that what I read to myself weeks, months or even years later needed certain qualities. I wanted to read something that I found beautiful and meaningful. But I also wanted to acknowledge that my grief was only a tiny speck. That every day before and since the day of my friends' deaths others have and will be grieving. So I wanted to make my poem universal. In the redrafting I noticed the images of death and dying, of loss and the notion of how an ordinary day can be turned upside down. How the world 'tips' for millions of people every day.

My poem showed to me a moment of realisation that occurred several months after the accident: that sometimes life is altered forever by events – not something to 'get over' but something that we need to learn to live alongside.

That morning
I went out early
while the frost
was still sizzling

and the trees
curled black,
like the feet of a dead crow.

A meteor,
fading
on its tired journey,

scattered ash
into space
and the earth tipped

towards Cassiopeia.

Close Up, From a Distance *Deborah Buchan*

> Through writing, we allow ourselves to move through the
> most important aspects of mourning – but at a safe and
> symbolic distance. We use our imaginations to revisit difficult
> experiences deliberately in an attempt to master them. We
> engage in searching for exact, concrete details and language
> evocative enough to communicate.
>
> (Louise DeSalvo 1999, p.56)

In any given therapeutic interaction, it is said that the issues arising in
the first moments will provide the themes for the rest of the journey. I sat
in my very first 'writing and health' session opposite poet and facilitator
Cynthia Fuller; and around the long table sat a number of women
of varying ages. We were invited to give our names and motives for
participating in the course. As we went around I heard one or two women
reflect that they had found themselves writing about their mothers, even
though in each case, their mothers had died some considerable time
previously. Each time I heard this, I thought that they were still 'doing
their grieving'.

At this point I did not see myself as a woman who had to deal with
'the mother daughter issue'. I said I was doing the course for myself
primarily, having worked for a long time in health and social care, and
that I now wanted to focus on my own creative writing process. I added
that I also hoped to learn something about the process of 'writing and
health'.

I did not feel the need to mention my mother.

In the sessions that followed nearly every poem to a surprising degree was either directly about my mother or intensely explored my own relationship with her as a small child and adolescent. This writing about my mother, who had died seven years previously, was done over a period of six weeks, in response to a variety of exercises, without any forethought.

One session particularly resonated for me: we were invited to choose from a selection of postcards and pictures and write in the 'voice of that person'. I was preoccupied with a portrait of a young girl. She had a sort of sadness or wistfulness and the colours were bleached out into greys and smoky blue. In my first effort I found a voice for this young woman, writing in the form of a letter, a device suggested by Cynthia:

'Dear Mother'

So sorry that you won't be coming home this summer
I wanted to tell you about the boy I liked
the mended swing in the old barn
I wanted to show you my pirouette
tell you myself and auntie had baked crème caramel

You write about the men who wait for you
outside the stage door
you say they make you laugh, that they
keep your spirits high you say
a man, a poet, has asked you to marry him
you've told him no, of course

I miss your warm breath, the taste of sugar on your lip
the white clean scent of soap on the cuff of your shirt
on your pillow the tang of your unwashed hair still lingers

In the garden my cousin waits for me
wearing his best suit and the tight smile he keeps for visitors,
for the point at which he knocks on my door,
by candlelight, in the eternal dread of night.

And I recognised then that a significant personal thread, very much about my mother and the times in my childhood and adolescent life when she seemed absent or unavailable, through illness or actual separation, was beginning to unravel. And I could see that my own work of mourning might have a chance of resolution, but through a fictionalised account. I then continued to write with this portrait in mind for a number of poems, until I felt that in some way this particular aspect of my relationship with my mother was sufficiently resolved, at least in the sense that I did not feel the need to revisit it.

Sharing the work was important, letting the material, the feelings and associations, 'go out' to the other women on my course became part of the process of integrating and resolving what losses had taken place for me. In this I felt that there was a second theme at play, following in the wake of grief and longing, to do with releasing feelings of shame and confusion, and the sharing of the material seemed important with regard to how I was successfully assimilating some of my lived experience, albeit in a 'hidden' or 'implied' way, at what DeSalvo calls 'a safe and symbolic distance'. Afterwards I was able to write more 'close to home' in terms of my real life experience, maintaining distance (and safety) by staying with the fictional: revisiting and further developing the first draft of a novel which I had begun during an MA in Creative Writing, then abandoned.

Any 'writing and health' process, I realised afterwards, offers a profound invitation through a given stimulus, the suggestion of place, a smell remembered, a sound recalled, or a picture. The blank page suggests an empty space – a field of potential that creativity and our own need seeks to occupy. What is there, inside the individual, is waiting to emerge and it may be surprising when it does come, having things to say to each person about where their real interest and any unfinished business may truly reside, whether they are fully conscious of the nature of this business, or not.

Writing My Mother's Obituary *Leone Ridsdale*

Writing, reading and redrafting my writing I realised it was both a reaction to loss, and a healing process. Pennebaker (1990) described this in his book on writing as self-therapy. For a short time it was also a displacement activity. Gradually I started to accept that my mother was gone; that I could not go on holding onto her in the process or product of writing.

The context for the writing was on the day after she died when I returned to her flat and piled her colourful dresses, silk underwear and pyjamas into boxes for a charity shop. I wrote the piece between doing this, contacting the coroner's officer about the autopsy, and collecting the death certificate.

Writing the piece and sorting my mother's clothes made me reconsider my mother's life and values, and my own. I had rebelled against her generation's orthodoxies. Emotionally I felt the need to bring together the facts of my mother's life, to create and hold onto a structure. But paradoxically I realised that my mother never painted her life as if it were structured.

I found and read recommended MA course readings, written in possibly similar circumstances. I read Handke's book on his mother, *A Sorrow Beyond Dreams* (2001). Comparing his mother's life to my mother's, I reflected how individuals conform to or resist the mores of their own generation, and how this is interpreted by their children. This caused me to re-evaluate my mother's and my own values.

A friend invited me to see Vanessa Redgrave in a play adapted from Joan Didion's book, *The Year of Magical Thinking* (2005). Didion's husband and daughter died in close succession. David Hare described the memoir as one of an over-controlling woman trying to master events which made her feel helpless. I recognised myself. The play was bleak, funny and reassuring: I was not the only one.

After the autopsy I read my piece to my mother. She lay in the purple suit I had chosen because she had worn it for her eldest grandson's wedding. I read it three times, and left it with her. I also wanted to give copies to mourners as they arrived at her funeral. I had worked as GP in the village for many years. The church was filled with people from different parts of her life. I wanted them to know about her whole life. Later I realised I was writing for me.

I wrote the first draft quickly. Finding time is difficult because I work full time as a doctor, and still have family coming and going at home. Revising was more prolonged; it was recrafted iteratively as I shared it with my extended family. They told me facts were wrong. I learned more about her early life, so the content became a family product.

The other reason for writing was my MA in Creative Writing and Personal Development, Sussex University. We were required to write 500 words every two weeks, and read it to our small group. I read the piece to my group of three women, and cried. Their feedback helped me develop it.

Here is part of my piece, redrafted over several weeks (edited later for *The Guardian* Obituaries):

> Lorna Ridsdale died at her home in Thames Ditton in January 2008, with her youngest son, Neil, at her side. Lorna was brought up at a time when women were expected to support men in their careers, but also at a time of great social change. Moving was an expected part of her life. Her parents married in their native Yorkshire in 1914. With World War I, her father, Thomas Peirson Frank, was posted to France in the Royal Engineers. When he returned he became City Engineer in Plymouth, where Lorna was born in 1920, a post-war baby, the second of five children. The family moved as her father became Engineer to larger cities, Cardiff, Liverpool, and finally London in 1930. He led civil engineering for London Council; this included building and repairing bridges, roads and utilities during World War II air raids.
>
> After Putney High School, Lorna went to Westminster School of Art, and when war began joined the ranks together with her sisters. Lorna started in the WRAF mending balloons; her sisters became drivers. After being made an officer, she worked on ciphers in Oxfordshire where she met and married Philip Ridsdale in 1941. Born in India, Philip served as a Reserve officer until gaining citizenship in the 1950s. Philip was posted abroad for the rest of the war, and Lorna had her first son, Brian in 1942. She stayed first with her parents in Putney, and when the house was damaged by bombing, took her son to relatives in Yorkshire.
>
> After her children had grown up, Lorna trained as a Yoga-for-Health teacher, and taught classes in Elmbridge, focussing latterly on Yoga for the less able. She said she 'inherited' the Old People's Fellowship, which met in Thames Ditton Parish Hall. She took this work seriously, making many friends who supported her. In her eighties she passed it on, but continued visiting the elderly. She played social tennis; her group of 'golden oldies' at Ember Sports Club arranged weekly games when their average age was 85.

Lorna was a cheerful companion to family and friends. She enjoyed socializing and had lovely stories about the quotidian aspects of life, which brought a smile to the lips. She took pleasure planning gatherings for her children and 15 grandchildren, with her own light touch. This continued into her last year, when she organised a 60th birthday party for one of her children at the RAF Club. After Christmas she flew with my family to Luxor to celebrate New Year. Here she enjoyed one of her favourite pastimes, lying with a book in the sunshine. Those who knew her will miss a lively presence. She lived life courageously and to the full.

'I'll Never Forget' *Joanne Robinson*

I had been keeping a journal for about 20 years but hadn't embraced the writer persona... I was a painter, surely they didn't mix? But what I found was when I painted first, the words flowed on the following page. I tapped into the source – the wellspring – and found the subconscious bubbled to the surface.

I began to explore my identity as a writer at an open weekend event on Knocklayd Mountain in the Glens of Antrim, provided by the Corrymeela Community, a peace and reconciliation organisation, working for 40 years in Northern Ireland. This gathering was facilitated by Damien Gorman: he would give us a few opening words and then we would pour out our offerings.

I will show three examples of my thoughts that weekend. Damien's prompts are in bold.

> **I'll never forget** the day Granda was buried. It rained so all the neighbouring farmers could come. All the men in their black coats and umbrellas standing outside the house and all the women inside. Granny and her sisters watching him being carried out of the house and down the long lane. Even when they had gone, I stood in my red dress and cried, promising to take care of Granny. I was fifteen and all these years have passed and I'm letting go, moving on, still tied to her heartstrings but feeling less responsible. Handing the baton back to her sons. I don't want to be a heroine, a martyr, a carer; I just want to be her grand daughter.

Hold her hand as she prepares to leave this world, pray with her to ease her worried brow. Let her go – to him who is waiting for her, her sweetheart, her husband. When she went out to work he made the dinner for her, when we watched the horse racing drinking stout, she sewed. I will always love her but what will I do when she's gone?

Cry for her or for me?

I'll never forget.

I am tired, very tired, but there is something I want you to know… I'm lonely, heartbroken, he's gone and won't be back! Tears roll and I can't stop them. I've thrown out all his stuff. Can you help me, hold me, tell me it will be ok? Tell me clichés, wives tales, something you think I want to hear. No more of my loves lies, I'm finally on my own. I don't like it, I'm unsteady, I'm frightened, rejected. Thinking makes my head hurt and my heart keeps on pumping. It wants love to last forever and I can't, it won't, it's broke.

Perhaps these two pieces are connected? Love lost and yet my absolute belief in it and need for it to go beyond the grave. The next example also has love at its core; maybe that's all I need in my life and these words are reminding me of my primary function in the world to love extravagantly.

We ran
In circles
On hot sand
Laughing…
I love you and I need you
To make me young again
Your spirit
Your imagination
You're more than my
Nephew
My friend!

I have found that the different medium of writing helps me reflect on my non-verbal expressions. I write feelings about an art work after I've finished: to dig down through the layers of multiple meanings it could have. Now I want to dance and sing as well and explore all aspects of my creative side. I think to address my own diverse range of emotions and feelings will help me in my work, life and quest for peace.

I started journaling as travel diaries, then found it was more about my experience than sites I had seen. I wrote just what I was feeling... and then after writing a while have those emotions changed?

Looking back through those early books I had stuck in wine and cheese labels, bits of fabric, stamps and other souvenirs. I suppose this is how I began to include art with my writing. Sunday magazines are best for unusual photos to cut or tear out. I arrange them on a sheet of card and glue down... Then I write about the composition, links between images, further things I wanted to explore, often just free flowing lists of words in response to the image like a dialogue even. I find this really helpful in discovering new insights and finding change has taken place bringing clarity.

CHAPTER 9

Managing Transitions

Edited by Kate Thompson

Transitions come upon us whether we are looking for them or not. Some transitions are inevitable, ineluctable life stage processes, others are choices or painful decisions. The contributors to this chapter make sense of their various transitional events of stages through writing. Judy Clinton takes an irreverent approach to the inevitability of growing old. She finds further joy and laughter in sharing her piece with friends. Gillie Jenkinson also finds sharing her writing is powerful. Her poem about the difficult process of emerging from a cult and rediscovering a self, elicits a poetic response from a listener.

At the other end of the spectrum Angie Butler writes extremely short pieces – only six words which can be long enough to capture some essence but not so long as to be a burden. They were her way of supporting her transition into a productive retirement. Mary Lee Moser finds comfort in stones when she faces various potentially life-transforming events.

Lynda Heines used dialogues to bring into consciousness things she tacitly knew about her ex-husband, so she could move on. Reinekke

Lengelle used a way of questioning her assumptions to challenge and transform her attitudes within her relationship.

Writing, Waiting, Rocks *Mary Lee Moser*

I can't go outside this morning. I'm waiting for three important calls: one from a financial planner about my money, one from the nurse about my son, and one from the hospital about the job application. Creased papers with questions scribbled in the margins are scattered on the kitchen counter.

I'm alone in the house except, of course, for the cats – all three are stretched out near my feet. I feel itchy and distracted. I look out the window, past our yard's mound of orange daisies and sea lavender, to see morning-grey cloud layers over a peek of the Pacific. I want to be in it, diving into white foam to clear my head, hearing the hiss and crash of big summer waves, tasting salt and letting go. Escape.

But instead of physical escape, I can write – always, always, always I can write. I have taught myself that *writing about anything* will help, so I will write about this purple glass bowl of stones and shells on the table.

Phone's ringing.

Not good news – but it will change, for the better – it must…I no longer fear the future.

I just realised I was clutching one of my white rocks all during that call. K. gives me such a funny look when I come home from a sunset walk with my mesh bag full of yet more of these small white stones. Maybe I will just write about this one stone: what it means to me, how I am connected to it. Why it comforts me.

This one's a pebble, really: small and flat enough to roll between my thumb and middle finger while I pick up this next call.

Better news about finances. Birds are chattering in the courtyard – three cat chins lift for a quick second.

Back to the rock: I see it's the exact size and shape of my thumbnail, but it's the colour – almost a non-colour – of these rocks that draws me to them, moves me to search for them at low tide in beds of stones of every colour plus this rare, milky – translucent but creamy – shade of white. I've tried to explain to K. that when I find them and pick them up it's because they pop up into my vision for being of the purest, brightest

white next to the black and brick red and grey-flecked beach stones –
impossible to resist! He just smiles.

It's only when I get the rocks home, and spread them out next to the
sink that I see them with fresh eyes, and I notice that most are not bright
white at all: they can be light yellow, greyish, streaked with a green. But
maybe one out of every 20 is pure white, and so transparent it looks like
cloudy glass. Sometimes a little sparkle trapped inside. This one on the
table next to me is like that.

Do I think it's quartz because that reminds me of the first rocks of
my life at Lake Michigan? My brother and me, on the sunny sidewalk,
smashing rocks of all sizes with hammers, delighting in the glittery
specks inside, calling Dad to come look at our 'quartz'.

Do I love all rocks because they remind me of that lake, of my lost
family?

And my son – two birthdays ago, mailing me that huge bag of
polished stones from his home two thousand miles away. 'Because I
know you like rocks,' he wrote, while I was thinking: *How much was that
postage?* I miss him – did I thank him enough for those rocks? I guess
it's not too late to re-thank him. It's really never too late to try anything
again. All less-than-perfect events can be corrected in some small way – I
have to believe this.

Picking up this little oval rock now, I'm thankful. For the calm it
brings me. I don't need to re-read or re-write what I've written about
this white rock; I don't need to know why or how the smoothness or
smallness or brightness of this perfect (to me) offering from Nature has
comforted me. It is enough to know that I have glass bowls and baskets
full of them here at home, and there are thousands more just outside – a
three-block walk, a left turn, a descent down the bluff path to the ocean
at the right time of day. And they will be there, among the dark rocks –
scattered white lights, moved by the waves, day into night and back…

Sometimes when I'm looking for the white rocks, I'll catch myself
thinking, 'I'm in the present moment – that's why I'm so happy right
now' and then of course right then I will have strayed from my present-
moment focus. I'm learning to laugh at myself for this, to be kinder.

It's the same with writing: the moment I think, 'What a relief!' is the
moment the relief is suspended, or dispersed. But then there is always
that free and clear choice: to dive back in.

The Door *Gillie Jenkinson*

When I wrote my prose poem, 'The Door', it was as if words and stories were emerging out of the mist of pain, confusion, shame and unspeakable abuse: both mine (I am an ex-cult member) and those of other people I have supported as a psychotherapist. I wrote in the first person singular, although the story is a collective experience. I did not know 'The Door' was there, hiding out of awareness, waiting to be expressed. It came about because my tutor for my MA in Gestalt Psychotherapy dissertation suggested I do a creative piece describing the cult experience rather than a dry description. I had never done this sort of thing before. I did not stop to think about what to say or plan it in any way. I sat down at the computer and wrote it in about 15 minutes. What emerged were different stages in a story as well as moods and feeling states which were depicted, highlighted and intensified as they expressed themselves in different 'voices' (I used different fonts, colours and staggered lines as I wrote). It poured out of me. A writer friend read it and suggested a few changes.

'The Door' is in two parts. The first part, used as the introduction to my dissertation, describes how the 'beautiful people' love bomb me and make seductive promises about their mission to make the world a better place via their enlightened and special leader. The sinister truth of what these people are creeps in as the door closes and I discover, with terror, that it is too late, there is no handle on the inside. Here is an extract from Part One:

> I wonder if the door is still there. I creep back, afraid to look; they may find
>
> me –
>
> but the room is black

I cannot find the door

I run my hand around the walls; there is an indent that could be a

door.

I remember the handle that let me in, colourful, beautiful, and feel for one the other side.

There is no handle

I cannot get out............

Part Two, the final part of my dissertation, describes the struggle after leaving. The cult had been publicly exposed and the door opened from the outside:

As I emerge through the door the cold light is too bright
I cannot see the hand out stretched to help
who can I trust?
Will I be struck by a thunderbolt and die as they said I would?
I'm weird, different now, not like everyone else
As my eyes begin to adjust to the light, I see kindness there,
how can they be, only <u>they</u> are good and kind…
in terror I take the hand outstretched
what if it happens again…how can I tell? how will I **know?**
I see acceptance,
kindness,
can they
have
felt
the pain
*that **fills the universe?***
I learn, step by little step, to do ordinary things again, the burden of

responsibility is off my shoulders, **the relief is huge**
But
…the meaning is gone it's all so pointless now, so dull and grey…shall I return…

I watch and begin to understand they did this to me and I did not know
I take the outstretched hand, I feel warmer now, and I hear the words:

I feel so angry that they did this to you

and finally weep for that little dot that I became

that was me

for all I lost

I understand

and safety grows – I can go on

I read 'The Door' at the International Cultic Studies Association Conference Philadelphia July 2008, to an audience of around 20 people. I put different voices to the different colours and fonts, expressing the terrible transformation from myself into this alien person, this cult pseudo-personality (Jenkinson 2009; Langone 1993), compliant, terrified and lost to myself. I felt emotional, it was healing to have my words heard; in a cult they are twisted, redefined and distorted, resulting in silence and terror. I felt a powerful sense of hope, compassion and joy, both for myself and my ex-cult-member clients. I have moved out of the misty darkness and so can they with the right understanding and support.

Patricia Cartledge came up to me after the panel and handed me a poem in response. I will end with her moving and affirming response to my reading – and my heart cries: 'it was all (nearly) worth it if I can use the experience to help others and grow in wisdom myself'.

Dear Gillie:

Your **G**raceful words
Lavish **I**nsight that
    Lightens the weight
Of our **L**ostness
    Inside the soul
Of **E**ach of us.

(Cartledge 2008)

Do the Work: A Writing Exercise that Turns You Around *Reinekke Lengelle*

> The progress of humane enlightenment can go no further
> than in picturing people not as vicious, but as mistaken.
> (Kenneth Burke 1937, pp.41–42)

If someone had told me there was a writing exercise that might prevent a bitter argument, I would have wanted to hear about it. Fortunately, providence brought me such an exercise in a book called *Loving What Is* by Byron Katie (2002). 'Katie', as she is called, was an over-weight, severely depressed, mother of three who had an emotional breakdown in her early forties. Her spontaneous recovery brought her this insight: we only suffer when we believe our thoughts. This idea turned into a four-question writing process called 'The Work'. Through inquiry and subsequent rephrasing of our thought or 'a turnaround', she invites those who are caught in a painful situation to write down their problems, question their pain-filled thinking, and come to discover that 'their story' is often 'more painful than reality'.

The Work begins when we feel angry or upset at someone (or at a situation). We write down how hurt, disappointed, or offended we feel without holding back. We are encouraged to vent and rant, no matter how petty we sound. There is even a helpful questionnaire called 'The-Judge-Your-Neighbor worksheet' that we can fill in. See Katie's website (www.thework.com).

My story

While spending a weekend with a girlfriend at our cabin, she and I got to talking about the different workshops we had taken over the years and she mentioned that she knew a holistic practitioner who she thought my husband might really like to meet. I immediately felt a twinge of resentment and told her that he 'doesn't do workshops'. As I said it, I was flooded by negative thoughts and feelings, that, in words, sounded like this: he doesn't like to work on himself; he doesn't want to learn new things; he should go to workshops; he should share my interest in health and well-being.

Although he had told me that he doesn't go to workshops because in his free time he would rather be 'painting' or 'lying on the couch listening to music', I found myself becoming more and more agitated thinking about what I viewed as his 'refusal'. Finally I grabbed my journal and wrote down a host of complaints.

Then, as Katie advises, I identified *one* statement or premise that I wanted to do The Work on.

Chief complaint: He should go to workshops (in his free time).

Katie's first question is:

1. Is it true? (Listen for the answer coming up from inside.) Is
   it true that he should go to workshops (in his free time)?

My first response to this question was: 'yes, damn right, he should!' This
YES was accompanied by evidence, of course. Evidence that was based
on assumptions, like: 'It would be good for him, because it's good for
me' and, 'He would be a better person or husband if he did...' or, 'He
needs to work on his personal development...'

The second question sounds deceptively like the first, but it asks us
to go a bit deeper.

2. Can you absolutely know that's true? Can I absolutely
   know that he should go to workshops (in his free time)?

I suddenly found myself not so sure. I wrote down, 'No, I guess I can't
absolutely know it's true'. (Please note: the answer to this question can
still be a resounding yes.)

The third question is:

3. How do you react when you believe the thought? How do
   I react when I believe the thought that he should go to
   workshops (in his free time) and he doesn't?

I am angry and resentful. I imagined myself going home and putting this
topic on *the agenda* as soon as possible. (This question gives you a chance
to feel what the thought is costing you emotionally and energetically.)

4. Who would you be without the thought? Who are you
   without *the thought* that he should go to workshops?

The fourth question allows you to experience yourself without the
judgement, if only for a moment. My response was, 'I would be me,
sitting on the couch writing and listening to music'. Note that I wrote
'listening to music'. I was, in fact, sitting on the couch, with my feet
up, listening to beautiful music that my husband had recorded; to my
amazement and shame, I suddenly realised that I was doing exactly what
he said he wanted to do in *his* free time!

As I sat there, feeling rather stunned and humbled, I also noted that
he had stayed behind at home to care for the children and tend to the
household. I imagined how my homecoming would have been had I still
believed my chief complaint instead of having a different perspective.

It is at this stage – after the four questions are answered – that the turnaround becomes possible. I tried on various alternatives as per Katie's format. Turnarounds are 'prescriptions for health' and you choose one that feels as true or truer than your initial premise.

Premise: He should go to workshops (in his free time).

Possible turnarounds

1. I should go to more workshops (because I enjoy it).

2. I should go to fewer workshops (obviously they haven't helped me become less judgemental, as I've just found out).

3. He should not go to workshops (he should be on the couch listening to his music).

4. My thinking should go to a workshop (it obviously needs a bit of adjusting).

5. I'm willing to have him not go to workshops (because he won't or because he's doing other things that he would rather do).

6. I'm wanting for him not to go to workshops (because that's the reality right now).

After a few more days at the cabin, I returned to a happy home and as I stood in the front entrance, I realised that the real trip I had come home from was my head trip.

Using Dialogue to Move On with My Life *Lynda Heines*

I've kept a journal (or what I used to call a diary) since the sixth grade – over 45 years. I've used writing to help me through boy and school problems, family issues, and later through divorce and deaths of family members. Fascinated by the importance of journaling in my life, I decided to read more about the craft and eventually became certified to teach Kay Adams' *Journal To The Self* (JTTS) class.

Since I started teaching journal writing ten years ago, I have found that one of my favorite techniques, the dialogue – writing both sides of a conversation – really helped my students find healthy resolutions to troubling situations in their lives, once they got past the initial awkward feelings of making up a conversation. Assuring them that they weren't actually putting words in anyone's mouth, but just listening to themselves, helped them to begin this exercise.

What I really like about dialogue is the flexibility of carrying on the conversation with not just people, but also places and things. In one of my journaling classes students dialogued with money. My breast cancer survivors talked to their bodies, church members had that conversation with God, and my retirement home participants held the dialogue with deceased friends.

After my divorce, dialogue helped me too. I tried to move through Pat's betrayal by screaming, crying, and writing unsent letters (and others I actually mailed) to everyone involved. I had used a variety of my writing exercises, but they weren't giving me the closure I needed to begin my new life. He wouldn't talk to me and I couldn't make him answer my emails, phone calls, or letters. So how could I reach him, get in that last word, and find peace for myself in this situation? Dialogue had helped me other times in my life. It was time for me to use this technique with this relationship.

To start this conversation with Pat, I prepared my journal page. I wrote 'Me' on the first line, skipped a couple of lines and wrote 'Pat'. I repeated this pattern to the bottom of the page. Having the names already in place gave me the freedom to continue the back and forth conversation without breaking the flow to write our names. Once this blank script template was completed, it was time to start the conversation.

Even though it is often easier to jumpstart the conversation with a question, I decided to open our discussion with a statement about closing my business, which had nothing to do with our relationship. Then I wrote his response to that statement. From there the conversation flowed from my pen until it came to a natural stopping point.

Me: You were right. I don't want to do this anymore.

Pat: You know I know you well. You can't seem to stick with anything.

Me: I would have stuck with you forever. I loved you more than anything.

Pat: Not true. You know better than that. Lynda, be honest with yourself – you love you. You're concerned with you.

Me: I'm, of course, concerned about me – evidently you weren't. I still can't believe you left, but more than that I can't believe we have no contact.

Pat: It just has to be this way for both of us. So much was said.

Me: But I was sorry for it. I forgave you and me and even HER. I just want to be friends, to be civil so I know there was something there. I want to know that you did love me in your own way, because I loved you in my very own way.

Pat: We've been through all of this. There is nothing else to say.

Me: But I'm not done. I'm not sure I'll ever be done with you.

Pat: You have to. I'll never change because this is all I know. You know my history – you know me better than anyone – and I can't change, don't want to, and never will. You are better off without me.

Me: I know that, but it still hurts. I still have that hole in my heart, and I just don't see how it will ever mend.

Pat: Darlin', it will. You are so strong, so smart – you'll make it through this time, too. And if you want me or need me, all you have to do is remember…that I wasn't always there for you.

Me: I know that. I just wanted you. But we can't always get what we want, but we get what we need.

After writing this, I paused and reread it. I felt as if we had really talked, and I realised through this exercise that Pat didn't tell me anything I didn't already know. He was right. I was better off without him. He wasn't there for me when I needed him. I was strong and smart and that hole in my heart would mend. With him out of my life, I could move forward. For the first time since that fateful day when he told me 'WE don't love each other anymore,' I felt at peace. It was time for me to move on with my life.

I discovered again that this writing exercise can reinforce what we already know, but also shed light on what has been resting in our subconscious mind. The magic of dialogue is that it goes beneath the surface, tearing away the evident, and bringing forth answers and insights that can help us find resolution.

Writing a Sketchbook *Angie Butler*

After early retirement from teaching, time lay heavily at my feet like a lazy dog. The time was at once delicious and frustrating, something to be valued and enjoyed, but somehow just not right. I found that after I'd tidied the house and got the evening meal ready, I had nothing else to do and ended up back in bed by noon.

Six months on and I began to have severe aches and pains and had to give up my swimming and daily walks. It was only after a visit to an 'alternative' kinesiology therapist that my aches and pains disappeared and I began to write.

My writing took me to other worlds, stole the languid lonely hours and gave me a purpose.

Later in the year I was invited to run some small group language teaching and enrolled on various writing groups. I used my link with schools to start my own projects, setting myself challenges as I did when I was teaching. These links have continued to grow, as has my commitment to writing and its value.

In the old days, it would only take a few words to grab my attention. A phrase would wake me in the early hours, land on my shoulder when I was having a shower, or pop out from a shop front when I was in the car. As long as I could jot it down it was safe, captured for when I could use it to inspire a short play, or a poem which would grab the children's attention.

Now my life has changed and moved on. The time dog stretching at my feet, is now a hamster wheel of demanding fingers tugging at my sleeves. The workaholic husband is retired and has stolen the 13 hours a day of being alone, which I had begun to treasure.

The elderly parents are even more demanding. But I have tasted the sweet taste of my own voice and that honey-coated finger tugs the strongest.

Just lately I read *Not Quite What I Was Planning – Six-word Memoirs* (Fershleiser and Smith 2008) and have found this a real source of inspiration and the 'notes' page at the back of the book is full of my own 'six-word' memoirs. The brevity of the challenge enhances its satisfaction for me, who is a so-called writer with not enough time in the day to write and no self-control to make time.

Words are still my greatest friends, whether I am reading aloud to parents, the adults or children I teach, or writing. Words share my innermost secrets, hopes, fears, joys and sadness. Each six-word memoir now captures the poem or piece to be written when I have time. They are the shopping list of my intent and serve a great purpose at this time in my life.

They have been a focus for writing classes of reluctant adult writers and less able children, those with heads full of pictures and dreams rather than words.

'I am not my mother yet'…serves as a warning and a reminder. How to be old and feeble is not what we intend to be. Annoying habits are not planned, and unkind comments made, are the result of frustration and inner sadness. Having sole responsibility for a difficult mother. My six words help me cope.

I wrote the following poem when two sparrows appeared on the bush outside the bedroom of my father-in-law the week before he died. The day he died one moved to the sill and tapped on the window. The next day they were gone. The six words of the title were scribbled on the bottom of a shopping list and shaped some weeks later.

The birds came to visit you
The birds came to visit you
They came to see if the time was right
From the roof top of your living
To tap the window of your death.
They waited together in preparation
On the top of their world bush,
Wholly visible to us all
Not a warning

But a gentle reminder that the time was coming.
One was bid to lead you
And came to the sill
Tapping impatiently
Like heaven's fingers drumming
And you tried to tell us you had to go.

A glance through my list of six words always brings satisfaction. Some will stand alone, some will help me through a difficult time and some will make me smile:

- 'She hasn't got time to die' about the third friend in a month diagnosed with cancer.

- 'Hanging onto ninety-three year old words' and, 'She has always enjoyed ill health', about the mothers, how different they are.

- Personal reflections like, 'I can't find my Feng-Shui book', 'Age shows when tweezers excite' and, 'My children have given me immortality'.

- 'Sex at sixty, what's it like?' followed by, 'It depends how you say it'.

And the favourites at the moment: 'Jumping into the Puddles of Life' hastily followed by 'What will lie beneath the surface?'

This way of writing works for me in my life and helps me in these days of high expectations and multi tasking. It enables me to lay down my sketchbook of words without it being an onerous burden, one more thing I haven't done.

I have seen the use of a few words, open doors for others and bring laughter, success and a feeling of completeness where none had been before.

And sometimes, just sometimes I have time to develop them into poems.

When I Get Old *Judy Clinton*

At about six-weekly intervals I meet with two of my writing friends to write together, eat lunch and share. One day one of my friends suggested that we should write spontaneously for 20 minutes in response to the subject 'When I get old...' Being menopausal, and acutely aware of the passage of the years, I wasn't immediately keen on this subject as it felt very depressing! However, I have learnt from long experience that writing 'just what comes' can be both therapeutic and revealing, so I was prepared to have a go.

Perhaps because I was in a frame of mind when I didn't want to be dismal, I immediately went into a humorous style – not my usual genre at all – and produced this piece (exactly as I wrote it, without any editing):

When I get old...
I'm going to become younger, as if I was growing backwards to perhaps late twenties, when I'd got past all the teenage spots and major hormone swings and felt that I could conquer the world. My wrinkles will smooth out magically, my muscles regain their strength and vigour and my skin will become clear and beautiful. My body will be supple, trim and a shape to die for, which I will deck, with my endless supply of money, with colourful, glorious clothes in the most select of materials.

My brain will fire magnificently with wit and great intelligence and people will sit mouth-agape at my untold wisdom.

I will bounce out of bed with tremendous energy and enthusiasm for the new day ahead, and my enthusiasm and ability to carry things through until the end of the day won't waver for a moment. My nights will be filled with blissfully deep and refreshing sleep.

My environment will be exquisitely beautiful – a glorious cottage in the countryside with a superb view to hills and trees. I'll have a large kitchen with a central table and a range and people will drop in to sit companionably around the table sharing laughter and good humour. I'll have a cheery, competent cleaner for the house and a cheery, competent gardener for the outside.

All my friends and family will be deliriously happy and wonderfully fit and healthy, full of excitement about their new project and ideas for the future. There will be no illness, no sadness and definitely no deaths. But there will be lots of new babies who will sleep through the night immediately and gurgle with happiness from dawn to dusk.

The sun will shine throughout each day, at a steady 70F with blue skies full of billowing fluffy clouds. Rain will fall heavy and refreshing during the night-time hours only. It won't get dark until 10.30 at night and it'll be light again about 6am.

There will be a perfect public transport system which will allow anybody to get anywhere at any time. There will be few cars on the roads. Canals will be re-opened, trams will be used again and a perfect railway system developed. There will be cycle-ways everywhere and people will wave to each other as they happily cycle along.

Nobody will be poor and there'll be no crime. We won't have any hospitals because everyone will be so fit. When people have had enough of this life they'll sit in a chair and disappear in a puff of smoke and everybody else will cheer.

Televisions, computers, sound-systems will all disappear and people will produce their own entertainment. People will play instruments spontaneously, sing exquisitely, produce the most wonderful pictures ever painted, dance in the streets with joy and laugh because they are all so happy.

Shopkeepers will bask in the sun outside their shops and give all their wares away for free. The shoppers will give the shopkeepers the things they want to have. Everyone will smile.

Clothes will wash themselves, hang themselves up on the line, iron themselves and put themselves away.

Children will play and laugh and co-operate with one another and grow into adults knowing exactly what they want to do in life and who they will be happy to marry.

Cats will purr on couches and dogs will take themselves out for walks. Cows will milk themselves. Vegetables will grow abundantly and everyone will go off eating meat.

When I read this to my friends (which we do in an unconditionally loving silence) we all laughed and laughed. It was all so ridiculous! But, it also made us laugh because it was a release of the pain of the realities that confront us as we get older. For that short while we could 'play make-believe' that we, and the world, are innocent and perfect. Later, when reflecting upon the piece further by myself, I saw how strongly I had expressed that which I value, and where I felt the omissions to be in my life. It gave me ideas and possibilities for what I might do in my future life, by my playful 'wish-list' wrapped up in my absurdities. Although I chose to write about getting old in a comic way, I had addressed the very concerns that I might have more bleakly expressed had I written in my usual serious mode. But this way we had the fun, and the healing of laughter as well.

I facilitate writing workshops for personal awareness and development, which originated from work that I did within Quaker circles, using Gillie Bolton's booklet *Writing the Spirit* (1994). These friends whom I write with come to my workshops from time to time. It is a gift for me not to have to facilitate when we come together informally, and also to be challenged by somebody else setting the writing subject.

I felt no need to edit the piece, nor give it to anybody other than a copy to my friends. It had served its purpose, both in the writing and the sharing of it.

CHAPTER 10

Developing Mindfulness

Edited by Kate Thompson

The Buddhist concept of mindfulness is the idea of being in the present moment, without judgement, without comment, and having an awareness of thoughts, feelings and sensations as they arise. The pieces in this chapter explore, invoke or illustrate this idea in a variety of ways. Not all the contributors in this chapter are Buddhists although some, like David Oldham, Ronna Jevne and Carolyn Henson make explicit reference to Buddhist ideas in their pieces. Others refer to mindfulness, taking deep breaths or the transience of the moment.

What links them is the deliberate encouragement of mindfulness and self-awareness and the move towards acceptance of self, relationships and environment. Ronna Jevne demonstrates this in a prison setting. Several contributors note how difficult or rare it is to find this kind of quiet and reflective space in the midst of busy lives. Janice Putrino recognises this through the dialogue she writes. Writing itself is one way of doing this but some people use a state of mindfulness as a preparation for writing. David Oldham uses his meditation practice as a precursor to his writing and allows his writing to emerge from the meditation, Elaine Trevitt also sees her poem 'write itself'.

Christine Nutt takes some deep breaths and prepares for writing by coming into an awareness of the moment without formal meditation. Carolyn Henson, Elaine Trevitt and Susan Wirth Fusco are all inspired by nature to reconnect with their inner selves, and to look for ways of understanding their experience. Stream of consciousness or flow writing is another way of achieving mindfulness in writing. As Julie Sanders reminds us this is a way of bypassing the rational brain and learned rules and settling into writing and the self.

Mindful Moments *David Oldham*

Breathing in – I am present in this moment, breathing out – I am aware of my presence in this moment, breathing in – I am calming my mind and body, breathing out – I am aware of my mind and body… Mindful meditation begins with an intention to sit in a comfortable but alert posture allowing the mind and body to settle but remain present in the moment with an awareness of whatever is present both in the internal and the external landscapes in that moment.

I experienced the moments written about in my poem, 'This Breathing Space', on a retreat which was designed to teach participants a mindful approach to working with pain and illness, an area that interests me on a personal and professional basis. The experiences and knowledge gained have inspired many aspects of my work and development. It was also an opportunity to take a little time out from a busy life and enjoy simply being on retreat, something I find to be healing in a broad sense, a wonderful opportunity to enhance my personal practice of mindful meditation. Often a sense of creativity manifests during a retreat and this is expressed in some form of writing, in this instance a poem.

So why a poem? And why this poem written on this retreat at this time?

Poetry writes itself through me. When practising mindful meditation I sometimes find that there is a poem within my mind reflecting the experience I am having. How does this happen? I'm not sure I want to answer this question: the process may well be complicated and difficult to understand, analysis possibly detracting from simply allowing the creative process itself to manifest. There's something magical about allowing the poem to unfold, letting it become conscious, being in the moment of creation and writing without thinking about it in any way, simply allowing the words to form on the page, feeling the rhythm through mind and body, finally seeing what is written. This itself is a mindful practice, has the essence of a meditative experience and is often accompanied by a mixture of pleasant emotions such as relief, wonder, surprise, sharing, giving and satisfaction. A real combination of these affects is something I cherish about these moments.

During the retreat I experienced precious moments on the cold and frosty wintry mornings, standing under the large expanses of blue sky, and in the evening looking out into the deep darkness of the universe, seeing the myriad of stars that become visible when in a place far away from light-polluted city skies. Nature's glories there for all to witness and feel part of.

The hours spent meditating with the group, the teachings that bring us into the present moment, the awareness of breathing, the benefits of mindfulness, the shared space.

These experiences enhance learning and understanding and come together in me as a creative urge develops to write. Time sitting quietly in the lounge, reading, thinking, sometimes just simply being. Smiles from those around and the many conversations that follow the smiles. The shared wisdoms, the sense of community growing as the week progresses.

This shared experience was enhanced during the small closing ceremony that took place on the final evening when I had the opportunity to read out the poem to the group, sharing from a compassionate heart with this collective 'union of beings', this 'meditation of minds' – phrases that manifested during the writing – allowing me to give something back to the participants in return for their generous sharing and giving during the week. This also has the benefit of a small 'confidence boost' as the poem was well received by many of the group, the quiet concentration as they listened followed by supportive comment and thanks afterwards, some requesting a copy with an attitude of warmth and friendly acceptance, which are now deeply appreciated memories from this transient community of kindly faces.

This Breathing Space
In and out…in and out
that's what this breathing's all about

and the delicate pauses in between
just to be in…just to be
me and you…and you and me
present in this place of space
with our 'community of souls'
with our 'union of beings'
with our 'meditation of minds'
in this space to find knowledge shared,
experiences gained,
and drops of wisdom poured…to be breathed as one
just in…and out…one breath

Writing a Haiku *Carolyn Henson*

'Go downstairs and out into the garden and write a haiku – and be back here in 15 minutes.' We rushed out of the university lecture room, down several flights of stairs and out into the busy Zurich street. It was hot. But a recent sharp shower of rain had settled the dust, and was glistening on the pavements and surrounding trees. I felt the hot air and breathed in the sweet wet earthy smell of the street and garden. Immediately the words for my haiku came to me. I scribbled them on a pad, and looked around and stood quite still taking in the moment – yes, the few chosen words were right. They felt quite precious, as if I had captured something in the street. I rushed up the flights of stairs and sat at my desk to arrange the words.

Traditionally, a haiku contains three lines of five, seven and then five syllables, making a total of 17 syllables. Currently, this tradition is modified so that no more than 17 syllables are arranged in no more than three lines, but the shorter the better. Being anxious at first, to get it right, I stuck to the traditional form and arranged my words accordingly. It was not difficult:

Rain falls in dry dust
Lavender lies wet and still
Rattling tram goes by

Then we listened to each other, as each person read their haiku to the group. I was amazed at the vivid quality of each poem, and the speed with which we had all found these words and arranged them. Only half an hour before this, I had not even known what a haiku was. We were at a conference in Zurich, exploring the teaching of Carl Jung, working in the university where he had himself been a teacher. Our teacher this day was David Rosen, a physician, psychiatrist and Jungian psychoananlyst who has written widely about spirituality and the healing process. My interest was both personal and professional. I wanted to know more about healing, and I wanted to explore my own creativity. I also learnt a lot about teaching that day, as we were given no more than about ten minutes introduction to haiku, and then sent out to write one and learn from the process and then from each other. It was very powerful. I have been writing haiku ever since.

One night, after my return from Zurich, I was feeling suddenly down to earth with a post-holiday feeling, and a heavy mood. I stood in my garden late at night looking up at the sky, and a haiku came:

Garden darkness hugs
Till high gaze finds – stars
Sudden sight, uplift

I was so happy with this haiku. My mood was transformed, and also my outlook and perspective. It was a healing experience. I learnt that the haiku helped me to relate to Nature and respond to it. A further need was to share the haiku with someone else, as we had done at the conference. The first stage in writing a haiku is the experiencing of the present moment, and engaging with it. Then there is the capturing of words that come almost intuitively to mind. This is followed by the thoughtful process of arranging words, seeking for rhythm and structure of some kind, and eliminating the unnecessary. There is openness to the essence of the moment. Finally it seems important to share the little poem that has appeared – often so quickly, sometimes after a struggle, but always, it seems, as a gift. The haiku connects us to others as we share some moment which has been captured and made meaningful by the attention given to it. The engagement involves one wholly – that is in body, mind and spirit. This is an intensely personal process, but it includes openness to Nature, to the wider environment and to others.

I sent the garden haiku to my sister and brother-in-law who had been at the conference with me and who had taken me there as their guest. The haiku was one way of thanking them, for it showed them how the conference had stirred up in me my own desire to be creative, and also particularly to write. I have since read the exchange of haiku in the book by Rosen and Weishaus (2004) and feel deeply affected by the relational process that these friends explore in a simple, yet profound way. It is not only the haiku itself that is significant, but also the short introduction to it, setting the context, in the same way as I described the Zurich scene and my night-time garden. This context is an essential source of the haiku and shows how the words spring up from the environment as well as from within the writer. The present moment is incorporated in a narrative, so past and present are connected. Haiku are essentially relational in several other ways, effecting a dialogue between outside and inside, heart and mind, conscious and unconscious processes, and one person with another.

There is so much more to learn about the healing power of haiku – in the work of Carl Jung and his teaching about active imagination (Johnson 1986), in the dialogical insights of Gestalt thinking which draw on the work of Martin Buber in *I and Thou* (1996), and in several world spiritual traditions, including Zen Buddhism, Shintoism and Taoism. Quite simply however, this is a creative process to discover experientially by engaging with the present moment. When we find words to express any experience we may diminish that moment, by capturing it in our own constructions, or we may discover a little of the moment itself, in all its freshness and aliveness, and receive the gift of its meaning for us.

Lost Heart *Elaine Trevitt*

It was the end of a grey winter and my mood matched the weather. I was out of energy, in pain and had lost joy. I had been working on a collection of poems about a significantly difficult area of my life. In one way this was enormously satisfying but I was also wondering if I was holding myself unnecessarily to the memories. I wanted peace and I wanted to be able to move on, which is why I was doing it. I had fallen in love with the therapeutic potential of writing but the question I was now beginning to ask myself was, 'When is therapeutic writing not?' It was a paradox I couldn't resolve.

Out in the garden the blackbirds were beginning to prospect for a nesting site. They clearly had a preference for some ivy growing thickly up and over a high wall, which I had earmarked for trimming. I knew that if those birds stared to build a nest in the ivy it would be months before I could cut it. Though I felt no enthusiasm for the job, unusually for me, as my garden is another of my loves, I was prompted, for the blackbirds' sakes, to get a move on. After the second day up a ladder with secateurs and shears (the blackbirds built elsewhere in the garden) I came inside the house, opened up my computer, and wrote the following.

> One day
> when she was clearing away big pots
> the gardener's heart fell into one of them.
> As she had not noticed she thought nothing of it.
>
> But she could not understand
> why she had fallen out of love
> with all her beloveds.
>
> Realising something was missing
> she looked everywhere for it
> but it's hard to find something
> when you don't even know what it is.
>
> Then one day when she went to re-fill the garden pots
> (new compost, new plants)
> she found her heart lying in the bottom of one of them.
>
> 'Oh my dear heart!' she exclaimed.
> She was delighted and stuffed it back into her chest.

This was a surprise! It was as if the writing wrote itself. I really had no idea where I was going when I started to write, and, because it was so novel, I knew that it came from a very deep place. Clearly the writing had information for me. It had something to say to me, rather than being something I had to say, which was the case for the poems I had been working on.

The writing re-minded me that physical work is a great remedy when you are stuck. It pumps up the blood but gives the brain a rest and in that space the brain starts to make different connections. At a single stroke it restored in me an enthusiasm for and faith in the process of writing itself, which I had felt at risk of losing, and my faith in my own inner wisdom, and it gave me confidence (Bluett 2007).

My garden is where I work out some of the tensions between wild and tame, order and chaos, where I play with texture and form. Whilst being no substitute for wilderness, it's where I create a little oasis in the city and a sacred space for myself. It's where I recoup and refresh myself and, because I do have physical limitations, sometimes where I also break myself. It has become a metaphor for my life. I have noticed time and again that what I do in the garden is what I do with my life.

I have a fair number of pots. They serve as focal points, and when I run out of ground, as I do, I can always do something new in a pot. However, container gardening is labour intensive and pots can be heavy. Over the winter I had been considering putting some of them away in order to make life easier. I had even considered moving away.

The writing told me that in considering curtailing my creativity, by putting away the pots, or leaving the place I love, I was making myself unhappy. It also told me that more work, not less, is what I needed in order to recover myself, that I should work in the garden as I always had, and to live my whole life too, with passion, almost recklessly, in spite of perceived limitations.

I felt the poem gave me clear direction and I took the message seriously. All spring and into summer I gardened hard. I did some big jobs that had been stacking up and, no real surprise, I fell back in love with my garden (and with some of my other loves too). I didn't have so much time for writing, but now I really *felt* the difference between writing as a process of self-discovery and writing done to express known experience. Another polarity to grapple with!

The pots in the poem are more than clay vessels in the garden, however. Earlier I had been exploring poetic forms and had discovered they make powerful 'containers' for difficult themes, much as a garden pot contains the roots of a rampaging plant. I had worked very hard on some of these formed poems and put my whole heart into them. Then without any apparent effort on my part, along comes a succinct piece of free writing that is unexpectedly also a container, holding within it the cause of my sickness and the remedy for it!

I had been reading Rumi, a few verses at bedtime every night. Rumi uses simple language and homely images to say the most profound things. My own spontaneous, to me almost Rumi-esque, writing about a lost heart in a garden pot was telling me that it was time to reclaim my heart. Time to move on. Time also to reflect on the value of 'containers'. New compost, new plants, perhaps. And, as usual, my garden as metaphor.

Loneliness *Julie Sanders*

Loneliness

The colour of loneliness is ice grey and it is a vast landscape the size of the North Pole with frozen cavernous spaces. Here there is no comfort and only ice cold water. I created this landscape myself by excluding myself from my mother's love and expecting nurturing from a mad man. It is nearly as old as me. Mistakenly I thought physical proximity was closeness and intensity was intimacy. I never felt lonely when I was caring for my father or my husband or my children or other people's children. Loneliness sounds hollow and chilling and it sleeps at the ends of the earth. It takes me with it into uninhabitable lands. It works hard to keep me isolated, with no way out, mesmerised. It is odourless and tries to impress others as purity or superiority. It meets only me and allows no one else in. Not one foot shall print on the smooth snowfall. It likes to look perfect and remain untouched. It hates visitors. In the past it was home to a whole wandering tribe who cooked, hunted and made love. Now it is empty and clings to the extremity of the earth. In the future it will melt. Loneliness will dissolve and reveal fertile ground beneath.

This piece was written in Le Val Dieu while staying at a farmhouse in the French Pyrenees. It was written in seven minutes using very fast stream of consciousness writing with no attention paid to grammar, spelling or handwriting. My writing flowed without stopping for thought, or preparation. The process bypassed my rational brain and accessed a pure creative energy. I found it important to trust the process. If I found I couldn't write, I wrote what was happening at the time such as, 'Now I've dried up and all words elude me. My mind is blank…'

I stole the format for writing this piece on loneliness from my daughter who told me about it after she had written a poem with Michael Donaghy, a visiting poet in a workshop at school. I think it works well with people in different phases of life. It is structured and provides a strong container for emotions.

I choose any abstract noun such as peace, happiness, wonder, silence, power, innocence, despair, hope, anger, meanness, guilt, hatred, fear, pain, etc. I then build up a concrete image of this nebulous abstract quality by writing descriptions using the following prompts:

> Its colour, its shape, its texture, how it came into being, where it lives, what it is made of, who made it, how old it is, how it communicates with others, what sounds it makes, where it sleeps, what work it does, what smells it has, what or whom it meets, what it likes to do best, what it hates doing, what it has done in the past, a journey it has made, what it will do in the future, and anything else I feel like writing.

Most importantly I go with the flow, write whatever comes, do not censor myself.

It also works well to focus on a strong emotion or reaction when I am writing alone.

I have used it in a more meditative way to explore feelings in depth. And I have written this way to focus on a strong emotion or reaction. I like to include any thoughts and feelings as they naturally emerge and not to stick rigidly to the list of prompts. I believe there is no right or wrong way to do this exercise and suggested prompts that do not resonate with me I tend to ignore. I use the prompts as motivators and like to be creative.

I feel this exercise also works well if writing with others. The facilitator in the group calls out the suggested prompts so that others can concentrate solely on writing.

I Have a Dream... *Ronna Jevne*

I chose to sit in silence in the quiet of my study, pen in hand, reflecting on the question, 'What am I doing? *Why am I going to the prison?* What do I want to have happen? What is possible?' It was not the first time nor the last time that I would use writing to clarify a vision of what could happen in a challenging work setting. I have learned to sit in solitude and wait for the words to come in response to the prompt, 'I have a dream…' At some point the dream will have a voice. The writing that results usually needs little revision. The process has yet to fail me. The outcome has always been a statement of purpose that serves as a compass for the work under consideration. With such clarity, it becomes possible for me to transcend roadblocks and to commit myself to what is worthy of effort but impossible to achieve. This time was no exception.

It began with accepting an invitation to facilitate a writing group at the women's prison. This meant that each week I found myself sitting with a group of eight to ten women who were initially unsure exactly why they were attending other than to fulfil their curiosity that it involved writing. They varied widely in intellectual capacity and educational backgrounds. All attended voluntarily and most were consistent, eager participants. They represented perpetrators of assorted serious crimes. Despite being warned they would use abusive language and that I would be the target of disrespect, not a single incidence of rudeness towards each other or myself ever arose. The only reminder that I was with incarcerated women was the obvious presence of a guard outside the door.

Every Tuesday I arrived with red licorice (a peace offering to those who were less than happy about being denied a smoke break), a selection of options for stimulating creativity and a curiosity as to how the session would unfold. Every Tuesday I left impressed with the power of their words to tell their stories, and struck by their courage to reveal their pain.

I reserved ten minutes at the beginning of each session as an informal forum for the women to simply talk to each other, an opportunity which is rare in the controlled culture of prison life. During one of the opening dialogues, a lifer asked me why I would give up my Tuesdays, travel three hours and contribute my time. My response to her was that I didn't yet know.

Predictably the dream did voice itself on paper. I began the formal part of the next session with, 'I want you to know you have in these few short sessions inspired a dream which I hope you will share.'

I have a dream. That every female in this institution, offender or employee, would write a piece that they feel good about. That every person would come to know that she can 'author' her own life despite difficult, even despairing, circumstances.

I have a dream that every woman would experiment with writing; would come to understand that it is not about good spelling and grammar. It is about knowing and believing in ourselves. It is about building community in a culture of pain and punishment. I have a dream that the pain could go on paper rather than be carved into flesh, or numbed by medication, legal or illegal. I have a dream we would find a way of speaking our truth to ourselves, to those we hurt and those who hurt us; and to those who imprison us, including ourselves.

I have a dream each woman writer will recognize the longing of another and gently encourage her to also find her voice and that we will become a collective voice, not of rebellion and advocacy but of change at its deepest level. That with our writings whether they be vignettes, or poetry, or starter novels – that we will craft a community of concern with our writing such that every women has at least a chance to someday say I can, 'Be *here*, be myself and be hopeful'.

I have a dream that every woman released from this institution will know her life story and have no shame, despite regret. That she will feel equipped to write her next chapter, that she will choose her co-authors well. That correction officers of all levels will write to develop themselves as characters who are instruments of humanity.

I know that when I leave here, you cannot. Yet, I know of many situations where incarcerated people found a way, not only of surviving, but of finding meaning while held in captivity, fairly or unfairly. I believe you are capable of doing so. And I believe writing will help you do so.

(Inspired by the EIFW Writing Group)

At first reading, the room was quiet. A request to have it reread broke the silence. I read the dream for a second time. Another inmate, a lifer, broke the second silence with the matter of fact style crafted from the maturity it must take to face life without parole for 25 years. Her words, 'You really believe in us' were echoed in the eyes of those who sat with pen in hand, ready to begin their writing session. I replied with a simple, 'Yes, I do.' And we got underway.

Although the dream was initially written in response to my need, I believe articulating the dream and sharing it deepened us as a group. Subsequent sessions took on a new tone, a hard to describe transition to a community of writers creating together. I was reminded of the Buddhist saying, 'Compassion is an experience that happens among equals.' There was no longer a them and a me. There was a 'we'. We were creating – together.

Conversation with a Ponderosa Pine *Susan Wirth Fusco*

How many times have I felt creatively stuck – bereft of images, of the words needed to propel me into that state of Csikszentmihalyi-described 'flow' (1990) so needed for a joyful, totally absorbing writing experience? Perhaps too many.

And yet, when I find myself in the midst of like-minded folk at a writing conference, creative sparks begin to fly, self-consciousness disappears, and the total involvement of my senses and awareness somehow pave the way to an 'un-stuck' state. At such moments, I can sense a glorious period of free-flowing writing during which I am completely unaware of time; of greater import is the sensation that I am learning something new or growth-enhancing about myself and the healing balms of writing.

Such was my experience at the June 2008 Power of Writing Journal Conference in Denver when I joined Ann Linnea, writer and wilderness guide, for journal writing exercises in the Colorado Rockies. This was a memorable, four-hour afternoon of writing outdoors: first, silencing myself, slowing down, becoming curious, and then, patiently waiting to hear the messages that nature had to offer me. Among the three different writing exercises given to the group, the second writing prompt required that I take one full hour to roam about the mountaintop, find and gradually introduce myself to a tree of my liking, then write down a conversation between myself and my new tree-friend.

While processing this experience after the fact, many group attendees pointed out that this was 'hard to do', that 'I couldn't get into it', whereas I, for some odd reason, was delighted to take a full 30 minutes to find my special ponderosa pine, then another thirty minutes to write down my conversation with her. I shared neither my thoughts nor my dialogue with the group; I was somehow overtaken with the effect that this ponderosa pine's words had on my psyche.

It was not until later that I realised how much psychological dust had been raised from this Rocky Mountain experience – dust from old emotional memories and baggage that had seemingly been laid to rest after almost 20 years of personal therapy and recovery programmes. Thematic material evoking a woman's desire to stay true to herself, despite struggles of all kinds and proportions, is manifest throughout the following dialogue.

The dialogue's unedited presentation here comes with no psychological analysis, no wistful commentary, but with a genuine acknowledgement that its impact on my being was profound, its meanings personally contemplated and fully processed weeks after the actual spontaneous writing experience.

Conversation with a Ponderosa Pine

Me: It took me almost 30 minutes to find you, but there you are! Anyway, may I call you 'sister'? We are about the same age, most likely.

The Tree: Why yes! I'll be your sister, whatever that is. Actually, no one ever notices me. This is going to be interesting… So… you think I'm sexy?

Me: Well, I picked you out of hundreds for many reasons. I love your young shape, not perfect mind you, but with a strong, erect trunk, lots of ponderosa pine needles and cones!

The Tree: Yes, and thank you! But I'm stuck here. See this baby pine next to me? She gets the afternoon sun, shading me too much on this one side. See? I'm lopsided.

Me: I noticed the baby right away! I only pray that you are kind to her, because you two make a nice pair. But I am worried about that nearby, ominous-looking older fellow on your left there – 20 feet higher than yourself, but slanting twenty-five, thirty degrees off-center, towards you! One terrible storm and that guy is going to crash right into you. Do you think that you will be safe during the next couple of years?

The Tree: Goodness! Of course, I worry about him crashing into me! I try my very darnedest to protect myself, to soak up as much water and minerals from the soil as I possibly can; I'm a fanatic about it. In order to grow strong, I breathe in good carbon dioxide, exhale oxygen vigorously; I mediate, soak up the sun, pray for mild winters – and try to live a spiritual life full of thanksgiving.

Me: I am duly impressed. Strange how I was drawn to you in particular...

The Tree: But don't you see? What I am most seriously concerned about is this paved road running beside me. Suppose some human folk decide to cut me down to widen the road? To landscape the area? What will become of me? What will become of my special energy, my softness, my inner strength – all vanishing in a flash of a sharp saw's blade?

A rereading of this dialogue underscores multiple paradoxes still simmering within. Who would have ever thought that a conversation with a tree could have aroused so much raw, personal psychic residue?

What did this writing experience teach me? As a trained therapist at this point in time, I do realise how important it is to remain consciously vigilant concerning the quality of my affective being on a daily basis; there is always personal work to do.

But when I *do* forget to keep this existential possibility on the front burner; impromptu writing exercises such as this Rocky Mountain High conversation jolt me upright into a mental, spiritual and physical 'Aha!' state of being – a state wherein I am reminded that I *can* train myself to let go of the self-defining, hurtful mindsets of yesteryear. On a daily basis, I *can* learn to live in the now, and to wake up – each and every day – with a self-affirming attitude that creates a sense of mindfulness with positive endorphins flowing.

Frustration and Me *Janice Putrino*

One particular day while preparing to teach a journaling group, I found myself feeling overwhelmed, frustrated, impatient and angry. I was rushing around to get my children where they needed to be, be attentive to their needs, prepare for work and my evening writing group and juggle the various other daily tasks. I wasn't doing well! I felt overextended, scattered, and very frustrated that I was not able to get everything done that needed to be done.

As I always do before a group, I reviewed the agenda and writing techniques that would be taught that evening. As I reviewed the techniques for the group that night, I decided it might be helpful to spend some time writing out my own negativity and frustration.

I started with a Dialogue, described in *Journal to the Self* (Adams 1990) as an exchange between you and someone or something else. In the journal, a Dialogue is a written conversation, where you write both parts. It looks like the script of a play. Dr Ira Progoff is widely acknowledged to be the founder of the therapeutic journal movement and the originator of the Dialogue technique as a journal device. Progoff's Intensive Journal® (1975) method teaches six types of Dialogue in the Dialogue Dimension section:

- Dialogue with Persons
- Dialogue with Events and Circumstances
- Dialogue with Works
- Dialogue with the Body
- Dialogue with Societies
- Dialogue with Inner Wisdom.

Adams (1990) adds four more:

- Dialogue with Emotions/Feelings
- Dialogue with Material Objects/Possessions
- Dialogue with Sub personalities/Symbols
- Dialogue with Resistance/Block.

I decided to write a dialogue with my frustration.

Me: Why are you rearing your ugly head again?

Frustration: Because you make it so easy for me to resurface.

Me: What do I do that makes it so easy for you to be so strong?

Frustration: You set yourself up for me by having unrealistic expectations of yourself, your family, your husband and kids.

Me: How can I keep you away?

Frustration: You already know the answer to that question.

Me: Why do you think I have all the answers?

Frustration: Because you know why I am here. Why do you keep asking why I've come?

Me: Because I feel stuck.

Frustration: Well, I am here as a wakeup call. When I come you are off balance and out of control. I am your sign that you have lost control of the balance in your life.

Me: So when you show up you are telling me that I am out of control?

Frustration: Yes, that is exactly it!

Me: Thank you for your honesty.

Frustration: You're welcome, now what are you going to do to keep me away?

Me: I am going to have to think about that. I need to make a plan to keep you away and stick with that plan. I will find a way to take better care of myself to keep you away.

Frustration: Good luck!

After reading my dialogue I was surprised at what I had discovered. I was frustrated not because of the demands of others or the pressures that I was experiencing but I was frustrated because *I* demanded too much of myself and others. After doing this dialogue I realised that I needed to make some drastic changes so that this frustration did not overcome me. Although I didn't like feeling frustrated, it was a sign to me, a wakeup call that I had lost my balance and reminder that only I had control of my choices.

This dialogue was a real eye opener for me. The anger, feelings of being overwhelmed…were present because I had set unrealistic goals for myself and was trying to do too much. After writing this dialogue I had insight and a different perspective. I realised that my frustration was a gift, a message to tell me that I need to stop, slow down and set more realistic priorities. I was able to take some deep breaths after writing this dialogue and my feelings of anger, overwhelm and frustration were lessened. I began to feel calm, hopeful and more in control. I prepared for my writing group and looked forward to teaching the dialogue technique to those in my group with the possibility of sharing my experience of my own dialogue with frustration.

Searching My Soul through Cyberspace *Christine Nutt*

I am lucky enough to have been meeting regularly for five years with a group of fabulous women. Our purpose (which we constantly question and review) is essentially to explore our Selves, our lives and relationships. We use e-mail to retain a sense of connection between meetings. Sometimes the contact is quite business-like but what is far more exciting and interesting for me is the use of this medium as a vital and enriching part of our group's process.

Before we meet I like to take the time and space to think about where I am, what's been happening in my life and what I need or want from the meeting. Using e-mail, I can begin the process of sharing these thoughts and feelings and put into words my initial thoughts about what I think useful to explore:

> I often think about our group and have recently been thinking about this meeting, and reflecting on those we have shared

since we met. I was excited and scared about allowing my shadow to surface but if it has, I haven't been aware of it! I know that I avoid conflict and feel this is an area in which I need to grow – the two seem connected for me: shadow and conflict. I'm interested in my role in the group, which may well reflect the role I play outside, of course, and also feel it would be interesting (if scary) to explore our relationships with each other – while we have H as a facilitator to provide the holding and containment – as shadow and conflict may have relevance here, too. The other thing which often hinders me is that I lose my power when I feel criticised, rejected or threatened – and I want to be able to stand my ground and fight my corner more assertively, instead of shrinking into a child-like place and withdrawing emotionally.

As our time together is limited, it can be productive and expedient to articulate our individual hopes and fears and to negotiate possible themes for the meeting in advance. This also offers an opportunity to reconnect as a group, so that we are more able to work at relational depth from the moment we meet.

I take time to reflect as I write, allowing my innermost thoughts and feelings to come into consciousness in a form of free-association. Elements of my internal processing that might otherwise remain buried are brought into my awareness and, if I choose to send the message, into the awareness of the other group members.

It is important to find a quiet, private space where I can concentrate mindfully on what I am trying to say. I breathe deeply and relax, excluding external distractions, coming much more clearly into relationship as I begin to write. My thoughts and feelings surge into awareness. Joy, anger, sadness, elation, confusion, pain, grief or fear rise to the surface and flow onto the page as I begin to experience fully whatever is happening in my mind and body.

Daniel Stern (2004, p.4) says:

> The Present moment does not whiz by…it crosses the stage more slowly, taking several seconds to unfold…[it] plays out a lived emotional drama.

I allow it the space and time and write whatever comes into my head and heart, without censure:

> … I want to ask you for something, which feels hugely risky… such a long pause, I'm lost for words here…how hard can it be to ask???…the rattle of the saboteur is ringing in my ears… Am I putting too much pressure on you, asking now, when I've said all that?…I shouldn't have asked…you won't want to… Do you like me enough?… Do you like me at all?…will you be able to say no?… Will anyone be really willing to say yes?… Aargh! Should I delete all this and just forget it, curl into a ball and withdraw onto my safe and lonely space?…

> … God, I feel so stupid!…and I've just realized I'm being quite insulting. I'm discounting everything I know deep down about your commitment to me and to each other – and to your selves, so of course I can trust you to say no if you want or need to. And I can trust that some of you will say yes. So I will ask…

Writing offers me a way of uncovering the elements of my own internal drama which would otherwise remain unconscious. In my own study, with only the computer screen as witness, I feel free to express myself without fear of judgement or recrimination. The process is cathartic, whether or not I decide to share what I've written. I am often surprised by what emerges and know that if I tried to articulate this 'in the moment', face-to-face with other group members, it would be difficult, if not impossible. I have realised over time that this is particularly true when I begin to feel ashamed. Writing allows me to forge ahead and say what I need or want to, especially when I'm struggling, rather than repeating old patterns of withdrawal and silencing myself. In itself, this is therapeutic.

If I *am* brave enough to press the 'send' button, the rewards are even richer. Daring to be vulnerable, sharing so openly with the other group members has deepened and enriched our relationships and offers an invaluable opportunity to heal old wounds as my struggles are met with care and compassion.

CHAPTER 11

Signals, Lines and Reflections
Writing on Trains

Fiona Hamilton

Trains are for meditation, for playing out long thought-processes, over and over; we trust them, perhaps because they have no choice but to go where they are going.
(Alastair Reid 1990, p.16)

Writer, you have longed for this place. An undisturbed, warm, light, place with a chair and a table, where your words can breathe. A comfortable room, neither too small nor too big, where you can be temporarily released from the world's frantic demands and dream. A space in which you are not required to – indeed cannot – earn money or complete tasks on a 'to do' list. Somewhere apart, yet connected to human activity, technology and landscape; somewhere quiet enough to think; somewhere containing plentiful subjects to replenish your realities and stoke your curiosity; people and places to observe as anonymously and imaginatively as you wish. Where is it? It is no ivory tower, library, garden shed or converted cupboard. It is the humble train.

Yes, the train. Perhaps not every train. Not the most overcrowded, clattering or dangerous ones. Not trains that are scratchy with chickens or pungent with goats or worse. But a train with a modicum of comfort and enough distance to cover for you to meditate and write – this train will do. I discovered this for myself when life took a painful swerve. I found myself having to travel from my home in Bristol to London and back twice a week to be with my unwell daughter. I discovered what the quiet carriages of Great Western Railway's locomotives, not a writing venue I had previously considered, can offer.

Everyone knows that trains are places for reading. But writing? It is often observed that the solitary nature of writing can take its toll. Not on a train. The loneliness of the long-distance writer is mitigated by the peripheral presence of others, the low babble of voices, the possibility of a stroll down the aisles for a coffee. Stepping onto a train, you enter a zone removed from life's regular demands and interruptions. Sit by the window and you have a privileged view of rivers, fields, trees, hills. All along your journey nature is in the ascendant and you are reminded that it, not cities and towns, is the wider context for all human doings. Periodically, tunnels snatch away light, inducing primitive fears. You re-emerge. From your elevated position the sky occupies two thirds of your view. You can gaze at the undersides of whole tribes of clouds: layered rain-clouds over Reading; bunched white cumuli clustering before Didcot; whisped vapour trails like afterthoughts near Chippenham; sunset beyond Bath, where corrugations seam purple-grey with amber and gold.

The train journey brings forth poetry – it *is* poetry. It takes the everyday, the mundane, and offers it up matter-of-factly while imbuing it with unique new life, illuminating it with meanings beyond. Surely Saussure must have formulated his linguistics, his foundations of literary theory, on a train journey? Where else do signs and signals so eloquently contribute to a system at once context-bound and archetypal? A green light flickers. Two hundred tons of metal move forward. At each station, the name on a sign in a standard prosaic font is both a statement of the obvious (*Where am I? Ah – Swindon*) and an enigma (*Really? Swindon?*). The sign calls itself into question as your eyes rest on it, hinting at other stations you have stopped at or passed through, other journeys you have made (*Yes, I remember…*) or that you might one day make.

The train journey offers an objective correlative for the writing process. The varying rhythms of acceleration and slowing, like the rhythms of language negotiating sense. The hypnotic hum of wheels on tracks as images stream past inducing a meditative state. The movements sideways and up and down, the small jerks and tilts counterpointing the primary linearity from beginning, through middle, to end. The parentheses as points change and one line arcs into another, taking you in a different, perhaps unexpected, direction. The intermittent pauses. And, somewhere, but not necessarily where you expected, the final stop, where you will re-emerge into the world, changed.

I wanted to tell a novel-length story. Could I conjure and sustain believable characters? Could I weave together the strands of a plot? Could I get the reader to want to turn each page? As the train journeys multiplied, the story started to reveal itself, and I began to feel I was listening to it rather than controlling it. Its demands and challenges through a painful episode of my life were also a kind of perverse relief – this was my alternative world, a project I could grapple with, a learning curve, an outlet for distress and worry, a different challenge than the one life had thrust upon me, a creative endeavour with pleasures and a potentially satisfying outcome. Each hundred-minute journey took me to many more places than the stops between Temple Meads and Paddington.

While an invisible driver took the controls I submitted to the process. Even when there were delays, there was the reassuring notion of numeric timetables, a framework for all the surprises, welcome and unwelcome, that happened along the way, such as the swan on the line near Bristol, who fluttered her majestic wings and refused to move, making a story later told and retold by the train manager at frequent intervals on the journey.

The train carriage was workaday enough to dispel romantic notions of writing as a leisurely activity dependent mainly on inspiration. I reverted to pen on paper as my laptop would not fit easily into a backpack and I didn't fancy carrying it during onward travel by bike. So my head, heart and hand worked together. Different muscles were exercised, both physically and mentally. Slowly, the story unfolded.

After 14 months of journeys there was a hint of change for our daughter. On one evening return to Bristol in early autumn I peered out of the train window into a dark exterior. An inchoate sequence of small illuminations paraded past: street lamps, the lights in offices, houses, hotels. Some were themselves, some were reflections. As I looked further, there were more: the neon-bright interior of the carriage superimposing itself on the passing exterior – a row of orange street lights marching across the back of a train seat and disappearing. My reflection stared back at me, surprising.

What I saw in this moving, transient display was held by the warm, vibrating vehicle that gave me time to engage with these visions, let them enter my consciousness, allow them to alter my perceptions and provoke a response. This gentle shaking of the senses, this stirring of the spirit, had, in more ways than one, kept me going. I had sought new combinations of words in an attempt to capture (*how can it be captured?*), describe (*who can describe it?*), render readable (*perhaps*), and honour (*yes*) experience. Experience that in the story involves a girl finding her way in the world and making several journeys, none by train.

The story has been written. The twice-weekly journeys are over. My daughter is home. The trains continue to run. No journey is ever the same twice.

Reflection

Writing this led me to see certain aspects of writing and my experience of writing on trains more clearly. It brought into focus counterpoints of light on darkened windows and surprising reflections. It led me to see the shapes of clouds, hear the resonances of the familiar station signs, and to notice other stories enfolding the story of my novel. I started to become more aware of deeper stories within the overt ones.

The train has no choice but to go where it is going. While writing, I experience being an initiator who very soon becomes a follower, a person with a pen and paper who finds herself, once moving, going along with a story bigger than – and in a sense outside – herself. I find myself discovering a story, uncovering it. The process feels both joyful and arduous.

I had no choice but to accept that my daughter was ill and that no one could fully explain why. There was no quick or easy cure. The issues were stark and uncompromising. In writing about departures and destinations, I became aware that I was also reflecting on life and mortality. We are all travelling an apparently linear journey between birth and death and this unequivocal truth had reached me insistently.

And there was another truth, no less unequivocal, but one that requires a particular kind of attention – that the journey is also not linear, but layered. It is not defined by a timetable and a departure and destination but by its own peculiar poetry of spirals and loops and connections along the way. We all have to get off somewhere. Writers must all put a full stop eventually (even e e cummings), but in between there are infinite dances to be wrought with sounds, colours, shapes – and infinite stories to be made out of those ephemeral and robust shape-shifting vehicles of thought, feeling and sound – words.

My frequent train journeys were not chosen but necessary. There was nowhere our daughter could receive appropriate help in the south-west of England. Writing each successive chapter gave me time in an alternative world that related closely to my deepest concerns, while simultaneously offering escape from present worries in their starkest form. The story was, in a sense, nothing to do with what was going on in real life. The central character is not me, her journey is not mine. And yet... she travels through uncertainty and makes discoveries. While writing, I was allowing influences from my present situation to play against and into strands of experience, both imagined and lived. The train and the frame of chapters provided secure and reliable, even reassuring, holding spaces in which the story could unfold. My daughter's illness shook the foundations of my world. Writing was one utterly portable, deep ever-unfolding medium in which to renegotiate the foundations and see if at the end of each journey I was still standing.

Many writers would rather be tied to a train track silent-movie-style, flailing arms and legs to the bitter brake-screeching last centimetre, than attribute to their writing to any kind of therapeutic effect. Perhaps they feel that it is better to leave the mysterious acts of creation alone, or perhaps that perpetuating mystification has its own rewards. I do not blame them. The necessary conditions for creative work do not sit well with deconstruction or bandages. Writers want life in all its diversity, perversity, shock and awe, not a tool for 'making better' or smoothing edges.

However, to say that the characters in my book arose unbidden from my imagination in a story that needed to be told is only one telling of many. While in some sense it remains the primary story in my relating here, it is also true that around it cluster a whole host of other stories. They do not need to be heard in the same way, but telling them may elucidate an aspect of writing which is about living and engaging with life.

Writing offered no bland, saccharine alleviation of symptoms but rather a passionate making and remaking, a taking pleasure, delight, an experiencing of loss, hopelessness, hope, a reaching out, a shedding, a perpetual enquiry. Losing ourselves and finding ourselves can sometimes feel like the same thing. Writing seems to me a process whose mysteries will not readily yield to our curious minds, although it invites and delights in our curiosity. Writing this has enabled me to see some – not all – of the journeys that were happening concurrently while I was travelling to see my daughter. What delights me now is that a journey of oil, pistons, a seat by a window and coffee in paper cups can find so many intricate, footloose and mischievous ways to resist being described, quite simply, as a journey of love.

———•◦•———

Writing Routes Map: Themes

Theme (other than chapter theme)	Chapter	Name
Ancestors	Chapter 6	Graham Hartill
	Chapter 7	Claire Williamson
	Chapter 7	Reinekke Lengelle
Bereavement	Chapter 7	Penelope Shuttle
	Chapter 8	Yvonne Watson
	Chapter 9	Angie Butler
Burnout	Chapter 1	Satu Nieminen
	Chapter 10	Janice Putrino
Childhood	Chapter 2	Angela Stoner
	Chapter 2	Myra Schneider
	Chapter 7	Les Murray
Dreams	Chapter 2	Juhani Ihanus
	Chapter 2	Angela Stoner

	Chapter 2	Tim Metcalf
	Chapter 7	Terhikki Linnainmaa
Family	Chapter 2	Shirley Serviss
	Chapter 3	Larry Butler
	Chapter 6	Nigel Gibbons
	Chapter 7	Les Murray
	Chapter 10	Janice Putrino
Health issues	Chapter 2	Andrew Rudd
	Chapter 3	Kathleen Adams
	Chapter 9	Angie Butler
Imagined futures	Chapter 9	Reinekke Lengelle
	Chapter 9	Judy Clinton
	Chapter 10	Ronna Jevne
Mythology	Chapter 1	Abi Curtis
Nature	Chapter 1	Abi Curtis
	Chapter 2	Tim Metcalf
	Chapter 3	Sue Glover Frykman
	Chapter 9	Mary Lee Moser
	Chapter 10	Elaine Trevitt
	Chapter 11	Fiona Hamilton
Reading/Sharing	Chapter 1	Debbie McCullis
	Chapter 7	Monica Suswin
	Chapter 7	Robert Hamberger
	Chapter 8	Leone Ridsdale
	Chapter 9	Gillie Jenkinson
	Chapter 9	Judy Clinton
	Chapter 10	David Oldham
	Chapter 10	Christine Nutt

Relationship ending	Chapter 3	Dominique De-Light
	Chapter 9	Lynda Heines
Self-harm	Chapter 5	Lucy O'Hagan *et al.*
Spirituality	Chapter 1	Kate Compston
	Chapter 2	Angela Stoner
	Chapter 10	Carolyn Henson
	Chapter 10	Susan Wirth Fusco
Therapies:		
Gestalt	Chapter 9	Gillie Jenkinson
	Chapter 10	Carolyn Henson
Transactional Analysis	Chapter 3	Sandy Hutchinson Nunns
	Chapter 4	Sue Ashby
Writer's block/	Chapter 1	Ray Russell
Finding a writing voice	Chapter 3	Francesca Creffield
	Chapter 3	Briony Goffin
	Chapter 5	Yona McGinni
	Chapter 9	Mary Lee Moser

Writing Routes Map: Types of Writing

Type of writing	Chapter	Name
Description	Chapter 6	Linda Sliwoski
	Chapter 9	Mary Lee Moser
	Chapter 9	Lynda Heines
'AlphaWrites'	Chapter 3	Kathleen Adams
Dialogue	Chapter 2	Angela Stoner
	Chapter 4	Sue Ashby
	Chapter 9	Lynda Heines
	Chapter 10	Susan Wirth Fusco
	Chapter 10	Janice Putrino
Freewriting	Chapter 1	Alexandra Boyle
	Chapter 3	Rosie Alexander
	Chapter 3	Sue Glover Frykman
	Chapter 4	Jay Carpenter
	Chapter 5	Yona McGinnis
	Chapter 5	Rose Flint

	Chapter 5	Rebecca Atherton
	Chapter 5	Lucy O'Hagan *et al.*
	Chapter 8	Deborah Buchan
	Chapter 10	Julie Sanders
	Chapter 10	Christine Nutt
Fiction	Chapter 1	Ray Russell
	Chapter 1	Sarah Salway
	Chapter 8	Deborah Buchan
Genre-writing (fairy tales)	Chapter 5	Lucy O'Hagan *et al.*
Journals	Chapter 1	Satu Nieminen
	Chapter 1	Alexandra Boyle
	Chapter 1	Debbie McCullis
	Chapter 1	Sarah Salway
	Chapter 2	Juhani Ihanus
	Chapter 4	Beverly Kirkhart
	Chapter 4	Jane Pace
	Chapter 4	Miriam Halahmy
	Chapter 5	Rebecca Atherton
	Chapter 8	Sarah Birnbach
Life-writing/memoir	Chapter 1	Debbie McCullis
	Chapter 3	Larry Butler
	Chapter 9	Angie Butler
Lists	Chapter 4	Beverly Kirkhart
	Chapter 4	Miriam Halahmy
	Chapter 4	Claire Willis
	Chapter 5	Lucy O'Hagan *et al.*
	Chapter 6	Glynis Charlton

	Chapter 9	Gillie Jenkinson
	Chapter 9	Angie Butler
	Chapter 10	David Oldham
	Chapter 10	Carolyn Henson
	Chapter 10	Elaine Trevitt
Redrafting	Chapter 1	Satu Nieminen
	Chapter 1	Alexandra Boyle
	Chapter 1	Sarah Salway
	Chapter 2	Myra Schneider
	Chapter 2	Shelley McAlister
	Chapter 2	Andrew Rudd
	Chapter 2	Tim Metcalf
	Chapter 2	Shirley Serviss
	Chapter 3	Briony Goffin
	Chapter 4	Bryony Doran
	Chapter 4	Claire Willis
	Chapter 5	Rose Flint
	Chapter 6	Glynis Charlton
	Chapter 6	Nigel Gibbons
	Chapter 6	Graham Hartill
	Chapter 6	Jonathan Knight
	Chapter 7	Robert Hamberger
	Chapter 8	Deborah Buchan
	Chapter 8	Leone Ridsdale
Sentence stems	Chapter 8	Joanne Robinson
Unsent letters	Chapter 2	Cheryl Moskowitz
	Chapter 8	Deborah Buchan
Writing and visualisation	Chapter 3	Francesca Creffield

The Editors

Gillie Bolton's research into writing for personal and professional development over the last 25 years has led to writing and editing five books (one of which is in its third edition) and a PhD. A grandmother of three, she lives in Bloomsbury, London, and Hope Valley, Derbyshire.

Victoria Field has a degree in Psychology, an MA in Cultural Policy, and has worked for the British Council in Istanbul, Moscow and Pakistan. She subsequently trained as a poetry therapist with the US National Association for Poetry Therapy (NAPT). She has received two awards from the NAPT for her international work. She is also a published poet and, as a playwright, is an Associate Artist at Hall for Cornwall.

Kate Thompson is a BACP senior accredited counsellor and supervisor and a journal therapist. After gaining a degree in English Literature from Cambridge University and therapeutic training, she developed a method of combining the two. She is a faculty member of the Center for Journal Therapy and Institute for Therapeutic Writing and lives in Colorado, USA.

The Contributors

Kathleen Adams LPC of Denver CO is the founder/director of the Center for Journal Therapy, where she trains people in the theory and practice of therapeutic writing online and around the world. She is the author of six books on journal writing, including the best-selling *Journal to the Self*. (See www.journaltherapy.com.)

Rosie Alexander discovered the therapeutic benefits of writing through her sporadic jottings while studying for a degree in English at Oxford University. Subsequently she trained as a counsellor and careers adviser and through her work she aspires to introduce more people to the power and pleasure of writing.

Sue Ashby, writer and psychotherapist, has pioneered Creative Words for Health and Well-being projects in the South-West of England. Her work brings together adults unable to access Higher Education. She works in communities with those who are isolated because of physical, emotional or mental health problems or living in remote rural locations.

Rebecca Atherton is editor of *Inside Out*, a literary arts magazine promoting creativity for self-development and emotional well-being. She is also a writer, poet and an artist. Her work has been published in anthologies, magazines and online. This year she is poet in residence for the London Poetry Festival.

Sarah Birnbach is a therapist in private practice in the Washington, DC area. A Certified Journal Facilitator, Sarah has been journaling for more than 25 years and shares the power of journaling in her workshops and clinical work. Her journals steadied her through grief following her father's death.

Alexandra Boyle lives in London and has recently completed a Postgraduate Certificate in Creative Writing Studies.

Deborah Buchan lives in the North-East of England and has an MA in Creative Writing. Her short stories and poems have received positive acclaim, and she is now working on a novel based on her experience as a teenage runaway and her time working with young people in residential care.

Angie Butler is a writer, teacher and small publisher of books for children, art cards and Cornwall-related material. She holds art and language workshops for all ages and abilities and has helped with two books of Land Girl memories.

Larry Butler was born in Illinois and has been living in Glasgow since 1981. He teaches tai-chi and leads writing groups in healthcare settings. Recent publications include *Han Shan Everywhere* (Survivors' Press, 2006) and *Butterfly Bones* (Two Ravens Press, 2008). He is convenor for Lapidus Scotland.

Jay Carpenter lives and works in East Cornwall. Jay wears two work hats, one as a community mental health worker for the NHS, the other running his own private practice as a Mobile Vibrational Therapist. He is also a member of Lapidus.

Glynis Charlton is a writer of often bleak prose and poetry who gave up project administration to pursue words. She now works freelance, delivering workshops and writing creative content for websites. Fascinated by the psyche, she is currently delving into her protagonist's thought processes for her first crime novel.

Judy Clinton has facilitated writing workshops for personal and spiritual development for over ten years. She has worked with a wide range of people, currently running sessions in a rehabilitation centre for recovering alcoholics and addicts. Her background is in teaching, social work and counselling. She is passionate about writing.

Kate Compston has now returned to her roots in Cornwall, where she has always felt most alive. Long ago, she was a minister of religion, more recently, a psychodynamic counsellor; she leads retreats and workshops on topics that fire her imagination. Her writing has appeared in various journals and anthologies.

Francesca Creffield lives with her children in Hove. She works in a mental health resource centre; part of her role is teaching therapeutic creative writing to adults who suffer from long-term and enduring mental health problems. She holds an MA in Creative Writing and Personal Development from the University of Sussex.

Abi Curtis is a lecturer in Creative Writing at the University of Sussex. Her poetry collection *Unexpected Weather* won Salt Publishing's Crashaw Prize in 2008.

Dominique De-Light has been writing since 1997. Her work includes travel guides, short stories, journalism, plays and fiction. For further information see www.dominiquedelight.com. Dominique is the co-founder of Creative Future, a charity promoting marginalised artists' and writers' work (www.creativefuture.org.uk).

Bryony Doran is a graduate of the MA in Writing at Sheffield Hallam University. Her novel, *The China Bird*, was published in April 2009. She has also had poems and short stories published and been short-listed for various prizes. Bryony is a Coach/Mentor for other writers. (See www.bryonydoran.com.)

Rose Flint is a writer and art therapist. She is Lead Writer for the Kingfisher Project, working with poetry in the hospital and community of Salisbury. She teaches Creative Writing for Therapeutic Purposes at Bristol University. She has four collections of poetry and prizes include the Cardiff International Poetry Competition.

Wendy French lives in London and facilitates writing in healthcare and educational settings. She has two full collections of poetry; the latest, *surely you know this*, was published in 2009 by tall-lighthouse press. The title is a fragment from Sappho. Wendy will be judging the Torbay Poetry Competition in 2010.

Sue Glover Frykman was born in 1953 in Yorkshire. Sue now lives and works in Sweden as a freelance translator. Published works include *Beneath the Croatian Sky* (Ebor Press, 1995), *Go and the Lord go with thee!* (Ebor Press, 1997) and *'Rite' from the Spirit* (Friends Fellowship of Healing, 2007).

Nigel Gibbons is studying counselling at the University of Bristol, having completed the University's Diploma in Creative Writing for Therapeutic Purposes. Currently he is using creative writing in a variety of settings. He has an exciting and vibrant family, and an attention-seeking beagle who has done time in therapy.

Briony Goffin lives and works in Cardiff. She has been teaching creative writing since 2002 in various healthcare, community and academic contexts, including Cardiff University. She has published widely on the art of teaching creative writing and supporting the emergent writer to fulfil their creative potential. (See www.brionygoffin.co.uk.)

Miriam Halahmy is a published author and poet. Three new novels are to be published by Meadowside Books (first title, *HIDDEN* in October 2010). Miriam was Chair of Lapidus, 2003–2005. Miriam is a workshop facilitator, writing mentor and independent editor. She reviews books and contributes to works on writing for personal development.

Robert Hamberger has published five poetry pamphlets and three collections: *Warpaint Angel* (Blackwater Press, 1997), *The Smug Bridegroom* (Five Leaves, 2002) and *Torso* (Redbeck Press, 2007). He has worked in the field of social work for 30 years and lives in Brighton with his partner Keith Rainger.

Fiona Hamilton is a poet whose second collection *Skinandi* explores landscapes, a river, character and how we make our lives with inherited, encountered and chosen materials. These themes inform Fiona's writing, teaching, inquiry and facilitation of others' creativity and well-being in Bristol University, NHS and complementary health settings and schools.

Graham Hartill's selected poems, *Cennau's Bell*, was published in 2005 by The Collective Press; 2007 saw the launch of *A Winged Head*, by Parthian Books Writer-in-residence at Her Majesty's Prison, Parc, Bridgend, Wales, Graham teaches creative writing for therapeutic purposes at Bristol University.

Lynda Heines' love of journal writing started in 1962 when she received a Girl Scout diary for Christmas. Forty-plus years later, she still keeps a journal of her feelings and life events. A Certified Journal Writing Instructor since 1998, she has designed and taught classes live, and online through www.heartwriting.biz.

Carolyn Henson has practised for several years as a psychotherapist. She presently works as a chaplain in a hospice, and also teaches pastoral counselling. She is a priest in the Church of England and has a particular interest in spirituality, which she hopes to explore and express through writing.

Sandy Hutchinson Nunns MA is a psychotherapist, supervisor and teacher living and working in Brighton where she works in private practice: teaching counselling students, therapeutic writing courses and women-centred psychology workshops. She reads and writes fantasy instead of doing housework and grows great garlic.

Juhani Ihanus PhD is Adjunct Professor of Cultural Psychology (University of Helsinki). He is a pioneer of biblio-poetry therapy in Finland and a member of the Editorial Board of the *Journal of Poetry Therapy*. He has published several books and articles on biblio-poetry therapy, literature and different areas of psychology.

Gillie Jenkinson is a UKCP accredited psychotherapist as well as a supervisor and trainer and lives and works in the Hope Valley, Derbyshire. She specialises in counselling those who have left cults and those who have been abused. She is a published writer. Her website is www. hopevalleycounselling.com.

Ronna Jevne is a registered psychologist in private practice whose career has spanned decades as a teacher, psychologist, professor, inspirational speaker and author. Her lifelong interest in therapeutic writing has involved students, patients, healthcare professionals, inmates and correctional officers. She can be reached through her website at www.ronnajevne.ca.

Beverly Kirkhart, author of *My Healing Companion* and other books, is a certified journal-writing instructor, keynote speaker and workshop leader for top organisations, cancer hospitals and national non-profit groups. Beverly resides in San Luis Obispo, California, as Director of the Hearst Cancer Resource Center.

Jonathan Knight is a full-time general medical practitioner in Suffolk. He is co-leader of a Reflective Writing for General Practitioners workshop held annually at Leiston Abbey in Suffolk. (See www.rcgp.org.uk/default. aspx?page=5555.)

Mary Lee Moser MA, Certified Instructor for Journal to the Self®, is the author of *There and Back: A Journal Guide for Special Needs Parents*, and an upcoming expressive arts book on resilience. Her Del Mar, California business, Create Today™ Journal Workshops and Books, emphasises the healing qualities of creativity.

Reinekke Lengelle MA is a poet, playwright, and non-fiction writer. She is a visiting graduate professor with Athabasca University in Canada where she designs and teaches online courses in the area of writing and personal development. Her latest book is *Blossom and Balsam: poems that reveal and heal* (2008). (See www.blacktulippress.com.)

Terhikki Linnainmaa lives in the town of Pori, Finland. She is a psychologist and a Gestalt-therapist and NLP Master Practitioner. She has been and will be a trainer of bibliotherapy and therapeutic creative writing at Helsinki University supplementary education courses in Lahti, Finland.

Shelley McAlister lives on the Isle of Wight. She writes short fiction and poetry. Her poetry collection *Sailing Under False Colours* was published by Arrowhead Press in 2004. She is a lecturer in Health and Social Care at the Open University.

Debbie McCulliss RN, MS, CAPF, CJI, is a wellness educator and Certified Applied Poetry Facilitator who focuses on facilitating writing/journaling/ poetry classes and retreats and writing poetry, memoir, and articles on narrative medicine. She teaches *Body Stories* for the Center for Journal Therapy.

Yona McGinnis is a yoga teacher and a graduate student of Pastoral Psychology and Counselling – Art Therapy Specialisation, in Edmonton, Alberta, Canada. She has recently facilitated workshops in community grief recovery and community art making using the Expressive Arts. She is interested in recovery from trauma through the arts.

Tim Metcalf lives with his partner Jane in the Brogo district of New South Wales, Australia. Tim is company doctor for Bega Cheese, and works in rural emergency departments and in general practice. His fifth poetry collection is *The Effective Butterfly* (Ginninderra, 2010).

Cheryl Moskowitz writes poetry and fiction. She was one of the co-founders of Lapidus and teaches on the Creative Writing and Personal Development MA at Sussex University. Publications include a novel, *Wyoming Trail* (Granta, 1998) and a children's poetry collection, *Can It Be About Me?* (Circle Time Press, 2009).

Les Murray is an Australian poet who lives in his native rural valley in New South Wales, between Forster and Gloucester. In Britain, his books are published by Carcanet.

Satu Nieminen is an occupational and bibliotherapist who lives in Hämeenlinna, Finland, working in the field of adult psychiatry in a psychiatric polyclinic at Kanta-Häme Central Hospital. She has studied bibliotherapy in the University of Tampere, uses bibliotherapy methods during her work and lectures and belongs to the Finnish Association of Bibliotherapy.

Christine Nutt lives in Essex with her two sons. A psychotherapist, supervisor and workshop leader with a range of other business interests, she loves communication and connection with people – both in writing and in person.

Lucy O'Hagan is a general medical practitioner with an academic interest in the philosophy and ethics of medicine. Lucy enjoys using words to convey complex ideas and emotions, and is interested in the power of narrative to transform the human condition.

David Oldham MA is a counsellor living and working in the North-West of England. He currently works both in private practice and in a day-care hospice where, as well as his bereavement and palliative care counselling, he also teaches mindful meditation and self-compassion and leads retreats.

Jane Pace is a Life Coach and Journal Writing Coach who believes that writing in her journal has saved her over and over again. She is a certified Instructor of Journal to the Self and her website is www.your-journaling-coach.com.

Gilly Pugh is a performing arts practitioner, has worked as an actor/writer/musician for the past 21 years, and has toured New Zealand several times.

Janice Putrino LMSW and Certified Journal Therapist is the founder and director of Writing for Wellness based in Rochester, NY. She is passionate about teaching individuals and groups how to use therapeutic writing to achieve wellness of body, mind and spirit.

Leone Ridsdale is Professor of neurology and General Practice at King's College, London. She was founding course organiser of an MSc for General Practitioners, and chair of medical student teaching in neurology and psychiatry. She adopted her children, and is doing a part-time MA in creative writing at Sussex University.

Joanne Robinson is Art Therapist for Ulster Cancer Foundation, having trained at Queens University, Belfast. Previously a fashion designer in Paris, Joanne has many years experience in community art-based programmes at the Corrymeela Community and L'arche Belfast with young adults with differing intellectual capacities.

Andrew Rudd lives in Cheshire and is a Lecturer at Manchester Metropolitan University. He was Cheshire Poet Laureate in 2006 and has published widely, including his collection *One Cloud Away from the Sky*.

Ray Russell runs an independent publishing company, Tartarus Press, in North Yorkshire with his partner, Rosalie Parker. His first collection of stories was published in 2009, and another is scheduled for 2010.

Sarah Salway is a journalist, poet and novelist. She is the Royal Literary Fellow at the London School of Economics and Political Science, and blogs regularly at www.sarahsalway.blogspot.com.

Julie Sanders lives in Greenwich, London, and works as a psychotherapist and tutor, having taught for 27 years in primary schools. She uses writing regularly for self-examination and healing, and facilitates therapeutic writing workshops using stream of consciousness writing and also writes stories with children in this way.

Maggie Sawkins lives in Southsea where she organises Tongues&Grooves Poetry and Music Club. As well as teaching at South Downs College, she delivers creative writing workshops in community and healthcare settings. She has two collections *Charcot's Pet* (Flarestack) and *The Zig Zag Woman* (Two Ravens Press).

Myra Schneider writes poetry and prose and tutors for The Poetry School. Her tenth poetry collection is *Circling The Core* (Enitharmon, 2009). Other books include *Writing Your Self* (Continuum, 2009), *Writing for Self-Discovery* (Element Books, 1998) – both with John Killick – and *Writing My Way Through Cancer* (Jessica Kingsley Publishers, 2003).

Shirley Serviss has published three poetry collections and co-edited a collection of women's writing on depression. She works part time as an Artist on the Wards for the Friends of University Hospitals in Edmonton, Alberta, Canada, and facilitates writing workshops for seniors, women, cancer patients and university students.

Penelope Shuttle has published eight poetry collections, including a *Selected Poems*. *Redgrove's Wife* (Bloodaxe Books, 2006) was described as a book of 'lament and celebration', and was short-listed for the Forward Prize, and the T.S. Eliot Award. Her ninth collection, *Sandgrain and Hourglass*, appears in October 2010, from Bloodaxe.

Linda Sliwoski MSN, RN, lives in Rochester, New York with husband Keith, and daughters Alannah and Lillian. A nurse for over 30 years, she enjoys bible study and quilting, is Certified Journal Instructor for Journal to the Self, and co-author of *My Healing Companion: A Journal for the Healthcare Provider*.

Angela Stoner is a storyteller and poet. She has been running writing for well-being workshops in community, education and care settings, since 2000. She is interested in using the language of symbol to unlock inner potential and her own poetry and her book *Once in a Blue Moon* reflect this.

Monica Suswin is working on her own book on creative therapeutic writing drawing on a life-time's diaries, notebooks, prose, drama and poetry. She contributed to the Jessica Kingsley publications *Writing Works* (2006), and *Dying, Bereavement and the Healing Arts* (2008). She lives in Sussex.

Elaine Trevitt has worked in primary healthcare as an osteopath, but is now concentrating on writing and gardening. She is actively engaged in peer mentorship, and lives near Morecambe Bay.

Margot Van Sluytman is a poet and award-winning expressive writing facilitator who teaches individuals how to write their voices to find healing and transformation. Her most recent book is *Sawbonna: Dialogue of Hope* which received high praise from Sister Helen Prejean, author of *Dead Man Walking*. (See www.margotvansluytman.com.)

Yvonne Watson has lived in Cornwall for 25 years. She has an MA in Literature. She is partly trained in counselling and psychotherapy but is currently concentrating on writing with her focus on poetry. Her poetry has been published in national and international poetry magazines.

Marliss Weber, a freelance writer from Alberta, Canada, has been published in numerous magazines, including *Legacy*, *Alberta Venture* and *SEE Magazine*, where she is currently Arts and Entertainment editor. She holds a Master of Arts in Communications, and teaches writing-related courses at MacEwan College and Alberta University.

Claire Williamson is a Therapeutic Writing practitioner, working in addiction recovery, trauma, profound disability and cancer care. She is lead tutor on Using Creative Writing for Therapeutic Purposes at the University of Bristol. Her publications are *Ride On* and *The Soulwater Pool*. She is currently working on a novel, *The Scarab Bookshop*.

Claire Willis is a clinical social worker and yoga/meditation teacher who has specialised in oncology for the last 15 years. She has taught writing in many settings, currently working with Facing Cancer Together: A Community of Hope. Claire maintains a private practice working with end-of-life issues in Cambridge, Massachusetts.

Susan Wirth Fusco PhD, LMHC, CADAC, CPT, is now completing her second PhD at Lesley University with Shaun McNiff. After a career at CUNY, NYC as Professor of French and French Literature, Susan is pursuing a long-abiding passion: researching Poetic Creativity and the Imagination as vehicles for healing.

Lizzi Yates is a visual artist whose work explores emotional landscapes. She is currently interested in combining image with music and performance to explore people's perceptual worlds.

Bibliography

Adams, K. (1990) *Journal to the Self: Twenty-two Paths to Personal Growth.* New York: Warner Books, Inc.

Adams, K. (1993) *The Way of the Journal: A Journal Therapy Workbook for Healing.* Lutherville, MD: Sidran Press.

Adams, K. (2004) *Scribing the Soul.* Denver: Centre for Journal Therapy.

Alvarez, A. (2005) *The Writer's Voice.* London: Bloomsbury.

Anderson, L. (ed.) (2006) *Creative Writing: A Workbook with Readings.* London: Routeledge.

Ansari, Z. and Field, V. (2007) *Prompted to Write: Three Years of Words for Well-being in Cornwall.* Truro: fal publications.

Auden, W.H. (1979) 'In Memory of W.B. Yeats.' In *Selected Poems.* London: Faber and Faber.

Berne, E. (1966) *The Principles of Group Treatment.* New York: Oxford University Press.

Bluett, J. (2007) 'Can too much poetry be bad for your health?' *Lapidus Quarterly 2,* 3, 6.

Boddy, K. (2006) 'Meet my sister the monster', review of *Moral Disorder* by Margaret Atwood. *The Observer,* 17 September. Available at www.guardian.co.uk/books/2006/sep/17/fiction.margaretatwood, accessed 15 October 2010.

Bolton, G. (1994) *Writing the Spirit: Material for Spiritual Exploration.* London: Quaker Resources for Learning.

Bolton, G. (1999) *The Therapeutic Potential of Creative Writing.* London: Jessica Kingsley Publishers.

Bolton, G. (2006) 'Writing From Objects.' In G. Bolton, V. Field, and K. Thompson (eds) *Writing Works*. London: Jessica Kingsley Publishers.

Bolton, G., Field, V. and Thompson, K. (eds) (2006) *Writing Works*. London: Jessica Kingsley Publishers.

Brande, D. (1996) *Becoming a Writer*. London: Pan.

Buber, M. (1996) *I and Thou* (trans. W. Kaufman). New York: Simon and Schuster, Touchstone Editions.

Burke, K. (1937) *Attitudes toward History*. Third edition. Berkeley: University of California Press.

Butler, L. (2008) *Butterfly Bones*. Ullapool: Two Ravens Press.

Cameron, J. (2007) *The Vein of Gold: A Journey to Your Creative Heart*. London: Pan.

Carson, A. (trans. 2002) *If Not Winter: Fragments of Sappho*. London: Virago.

Cartledge, P. (2008) Personal communication.

Chanan, G., Mills, R., Ntuli, P. and Presley, F. (eds) (1989) *Affirming Flame*. London: Community Projects Foundation.

Clarkson, P. (2008) *The Therapeutic Relationship*. London: Whurr.

Csikszentmihalyi, M. (1990) *Flow: The Psychology of Optimal Experience*. New York: Harper Collins.

Cuddon, J.A. (1976) *A Dictionary of Literary Terms*. New York: Doubleday.

DeSalvo, L. (1999) *Writing as a Way of Healing*. Boston: Beacon Press.

Didion, J. (2005) *The Year of Magical Thinking*. London: Random House.

Erskine, R. and Zalcman, M. (1979) 'The Racket System: A model for Racket Analysis.' *TA Journal 9*, 1, 51–59.

Etherington, K. (2004) Becoming a Reflexive Researcher. London: Jessica Kingsley Publishers.

Fershleiser, R. and Smith, L. (2008) *Not Quite What I Was Planning: Six-word Memoirs*. New York: Harper Collins.

Flint, R. (2003) 'The Blue Gate.' In *Nekyia*. Exeter: Stride.

Ford, D. (1998) *The Dark Side of The Light Chasers: Reclaiming Your Power, Creativity, Brilliance and Dreams*. London: Hodder and Stoughton.

Freed, R. (2003) *Women's Lives, Women's Legacies: Passing Your Beliefs and Blessings to Future Generations*. Minneapolis: Fairview Press.

Freud, S. (1899/1997) *The Interpretation of Dreams*. Ware: Wordsworth Editions Ltd.

Gallagher, T. (1995) 'Black Silk.' In My Black Horse: New and Selected Poems. Tarset, Northumberland: Bloodaxe Books.

Gillies, A. (2009) 'Alzheimer's takes away our memory and our selves.' *The Times*, 18 November. Available at www.timesonline.co.uk, accessed 18 February 2010.

Glover Frykman, S. (2007) *Rite from the Spirit.* London: Friends Fellowship of Healing.

Goldberg, N. (1986) *Writing Down the Bones.* Boston: Shambhala.

Goulding, R. and Goulding, M. (1976) 'Injunctions, decisions and redecisions.' *Transactional Journal 6*, 1, 41–48.

Gueber, H. A. (1994) *Greece and Rome: Myths and Legends.* London: Senate.

Hamberger, R. (2002) *The Smug Bridegroom.* Nottingham: Five Leaves Publications.

Handke, P. (2001) *A Sorrow Beyond Dreams* (trans. R. Manheim). London: Pushkin Press.

Hartill, G. (2005) *Cennau's Bell, Poems 1980–2001.* Abergavenny: The Collective Press.

Heffron, J. (2000) *The Writer's Idea Book.* Cincinnati, Ohio: Writer's Digest Books.

Hellinger, B. (1998) *Love's Hidden Symmetry: What makes Love Work in Relationships.* Phoenix, Arizona: Zeig Tucker and Co.

Hellinger, B. (2001) 'Introduction to Family Constellations.' Lecture and Demonstration in Taipei on 11 October 2001. Available at www.hellinger.co.uk, accessed 25 September 2010.

Hirsch, E. (1999) How to Read a Poem. San Diego: Harcourt.

Hopkins, G.M. (1985) *Poems and Prose* (ed. W.H.Gardner). London: Penguin.

Hopkins, G.M. (2002) *The Major Works.* Oxford: Oxford World Classics.

Hughes, T. (1967) *Poetry in the Making.* London: Faber and Faber.

Hycner, R. (1991) *Between Person and Person: Toward a Dialogical Psychotherapy.* Highland, NY: The Gestalt Journal Press.

Hynes, A.M. and Hynes-Berry, M. (1994) *Biblio/Poetry Therapy: The Interactive Process: A Handbook.* St Cloud, MN: North Star Press.

Jenkinson, G.M. (2009) 'An investigation into cult pseudo-personality: What is it and how does it form?' *Cultic Studies Review 7*, 3, 199–244. Available at www.icsahome.org, accessed 16 June 2010.

Johnson, R.A. (1986) *Inner Work: Using Dreams and Active Imagination for Personal Growth.* San Francisco: Harper.

Kahler, T. and Capers, H. (1974) 'The miniscript.' *Transactional Journal 4*, 1, 26–42.

Katie, B. (2002) *Loving What Is: Four Questions that can Change Your Life.* New York: Harmony Books.

Kirkhart, B.K. (2008) *My Healing Companion.* Ann Arbor: Comeback Press Inc.

Kiteley, B. (2005) *The 3 A.M. Epiphany: Uncommon Writing Exercises That Transform Your Fiction.* Cincinnati, Ohio: Writer's Digest Books.

Langone, M.D. (ed.) (1993) *Recovery From Cults, Help for Victims of Psychological and Spiritual Abuse.* New York: W.W. Norton and Company.

Levertov, D. (1967) *Poems 1960–1967.* New York: New Directions Publishing Corporation.

McAlister, S. (2004) 'Dr Shelley.' *The Rialto 56,* 50.

Merwin, W.S. (2008) *The Shadow of Sirius.* Port Townsend, WA: Copper Canyon Press.

Moskowitz, C. (2010) *Letter to the Man at Journal Square Station.* US literary online journal: *Drunken Boat,* no.11. Available at www.drunkenboat.com, accessed 16 June 2010.

Munno, A. (2006) 'A complaint that changed my practice.' *British Medical Journal 332,* 1092.

Murray, L. (1998) 'Burning Want.' In *Collected Poems.* Manchester: Carcanet.

Olds, S. (2005) *Selected Poems.* London: Cape.

Padel, R. (2007) *The Poem and the Journey.* London: Chatto and Windus.

Passons, W.R. (1975) *Gestalt Approaches in Counselling.* New York: Holt, Rinehart and Winston Inc.

Paterson, D. (ed.) (1999) *101 Sonnets from Shakespeare to Heaney.* London: Faber and Faber.

Pennebaker, J.W. (1990) *Opening Up: The Healing Powers of Expressing Emotions.* New York: The Guildford Press.

Progoff, I. (1975) *At a Journal Workshop.* New York: Dialogue House.

Redgrove, P. (2006) 'The Harper.' In *The Harper.* London: Jonathan Cape

Reid, A. (1990) *Whereabouts: Notes on Being a Foreigner.* New York: White Pine Press.

Ridsdale, L. (2008) 'Other lives: Lorna Ridsdale.' *The Guardian,* 6 March 2008, p.37.

Rosen, D. (2002) *Transforming Depression: Healing the Soul through Creativity.* York Beach, Maine: Nicolas-Hays.

Rosen, D. and Weishaus, J. (2004) *The Healing Spirit of Haiku.* Berkeley, California: North Atlantic Books.

Rudd, A. (2007) *One Cloud Away from the Sky.* Chester: Cheshire County Council.

Rumi (1995) *The Essential Rumi* (trans. C. Barks and J. Moyne). New York: Harper Collins.

Sawkins, M. (2008) 'The Year The Wall Came Down.' *Brittle Star,* issue 21, Winter, London.

Schneider, M. (2008) *Circling the Core.* London: Enitharmon Press.

Schneider, M. and Killick, J. (1998) Writing For Self Discovery. Shaftesbury: Element Books.

Segalove, I. (2004) *40 Days and 40 Nights: Taking Time Out for Self Discovery, A Guided Journal.* Kansas, MS: Andrew McMeel Publishing.

Serviss, S. (1992) *Model Families.* Edmonton: Rowan Books.

Stern, D.N. (2004) *The Present Moment in Psychotherapy and Everyday Life.* New York: W.W. Norton and Company.

Stewart, I. and Joines, V. (1987) *TA Today: A New Introduction to Transactional Analysis.* Nottingham: Lifespace Publishing.

Ulsamer, B. (2005) *The Healing Power of the Past: The Systematic Therapy of Bert Hellinger.* Nevada City, California: Underwood Books.

Woollams, S. and Brown, M. (1978) *Transactional Analysis: A Modern and Comprehensive Text of TA Theory and Practice.* Huron Valley: Institute Press.

Yontef, G. (1993) *Awareness, Dialogue, and Process.* New York: The Gestalt Journal Press.